GOD,
FREEDOM,
and EVIL

GOD,
FREEDOM,
and EVIL

Alvin Plantinga

William B. Eerdmans Publishing Company

Reprinted, August 1991

Library of Congress Cataloging in Publication Data

Plantinga, Alvin.
    God, freedom, and evil.

    Reprint of the ed. published by Harper & Row, New York, issued in series: Basic conditions of life as TB 1811 of Harper torchbooks.
    Includes bibliographical references.
    1. God — Proof.   2. Good and evil.   3. Theodicy.
I. Title.
[BT102.P56   1978]   216   77-17218
ISBN 0-8028-1731-9

To the memory of Ophelia Baarman, Chris Baarman,
and Gertrude Postma

Table of Contents

GOD, FREEDOM, and EVIL

Introduction

This book discusses and exemplifies the philosophy of religion, or philosophical reflection on central themes of religion. Philosophical reflection (which is not much different from just thinking hard) on these themes has a long history: it dates back at least as far as the fifth century B.C. when some of the Greeks thought long and hard about the religion they had received from their ancestors. In the Christian era such philosophical reflection begins in the first or second century with the early church fathers, or "Patristics" as they are often called; it has continued ever since.

The heart of many of the major religions—Christianity, Judaism, Islam, for example—is belief in God. Of course these religions—*theistic* religions—differ among themselves as to how they conceive of God. The Christian tradition, for example, emphasizes God's love and benevolence; in the Moslem view, on the other hand, God has a somewhat more arbitrary character. There are also supersophisticates among allegedly Christian theologians who proclaim the liberation of Christianity from belief in God, seeking to replace it by trust in "Being itself" or the "Ground of Being" or some such thing. But for the most part it remains true that belief in God is the foundation of these great religions.

Now belief *in* God is not the same thing as belief that God exists, or that there *is* such a thing as God. To believe that God exists is simply to accept a proposition of a certain sort—a proposition affirming that there is a personal being who, let's say, has existed from eternity, is almighty, perfectly wise, perfectly just, has created the world, and loves his creatures. To believe *in* God, however, is quite another matter. The Apostle's Creed begins thus: "I believe in God the Father Almighty, Maker of Heaven and earth. . . ." One who repeats these words and means what he says is not simply announcing the fact that he accepts a certain proposition as true; much more is involved than that. Belief in God means *trusting* God, accepting Him, committing one's life to Him. To the believer the entire world looks different. Blue sky, verdant forests, great mountains, surging ocean, friends and family, love in its many forms and various manifestations—the believer sees these things as gifts from God. The entire universe takes on a personal cast for him; the fundamental truth about reality is truth about a *Person.* So believing in God is more than accepting the proposition that God exists. Still, it is at least that much. One can't sensibly believe in God and thank Him for the mountains without believing that there *is* such a person to be thanked, and that He is in some way responsible for the mountains. Nor can one trust in God and commit oneself to Him without believing that He exists: "He who would come to God must believe that he is, and that he is a rewarder of those who seek him" (Heb. 11: 6).

One important aspect of philosophy of religion concerns this latter belief—the belief that God exists, that there really is a being of the sort theists claim to worship and trust. This belief, however, has not been universally accepted. Many have rejected it; some have claimed that it is plainly false and that it is irrational to accept it. By way of response some theologians and theistic philosophers have tried to give successful arguments or *proofs* for the existence of God. This enterprise is called *natural theology.* The natural theologian does not, typically, offer his arguments in order to convince people of God's existence; and in fact few who accept theistic belief do so because they find such an argument compelling. Instead the typical function of natural theology has been to show that religious belief is rationally acceptable. Other philosophers, of course, have presented arguments for the *falsehood* of theistic beliefs;

these philosophers conclude that belief in God is demonstrably irrational or unreasonable. We might call this enterprise *natural atheology.*

One area of philosophy of religion, then, inquires into the rational acceptability of theistic belief. Here we examine the arguments of natural theology and natural atheology. We ask whether any of these arguments are successful and whether any provides either proof of or evidence for its conclusion. Of course this topic is not the only one in philosophy of religion, but it is an important one and one upon which this book will concentrate.

Of course this topic—the rationality of theistic belief—is not restricted to philosophy or philosophers. It plays a prominent role in literature—in Milton's *Paradise Lost,* for example, as well as in Dostoevski's *The Brothers Karamazov,* and in some of Thomas Hardy's novels. This same theme may be found in the works of many more recent authors—for example, Gerard Manley Hopkins, T. S. Eliot, Peter De Vries, and, perhaps, John Updike. And it may be difficult, if not impossible, to give a clear and useful definition of the philosophical, as opposed, say, to the literary way of approaching this theme. It is also unnecessary. A much better way to get a feel for the philosophical approach is to examine some representative samples. This book is such a sample. In discussing subjects of natural theology and natural atheology I shall not adopt a pose of fine impartiality; instead I shall comment in detail on some of the main points and spell out what appears to me to be the truth of the matter. But I shall not try to say something about every important argument or about every topic that arises in connection with those I do discuss; to do that would be to say much too little about any. Instead I shall concentrate my comments upon just two of the traditional arguments: the ontological argument as an example of natural theology and the problem of evil as the most important representative of natural atheology. (What I have to say on some of the remaining topics and arguments can be found in *God and Other Minds* [Ithaca, N.Y.: Cornell University Press, 1967].) I believe that some recently won insights in the philosophy of logic—particularly those centering about the idea of *possible worlds*—genuinely illumine these classical topics; a moderately innovative feature of this book, therefore, is my attempt to show how these insights throw light upon these topics. Much of the material developed in this book can be found in more rigorous and complete form in my book *The Nature of Necessity* (Oxford: The Clarendon Press, 1974).

I have tried to put what I have to say in a way that is philosophically accurate and responsible; but I have tried especially hard to put it as clearly and simply as the subject allows. These great topics are of interest and concern to many—not just professional philosophers and theologians. So I hope this book will be useful to the philosophical novice and to the fabled general reader. All it will require, I hope, is a determination to follow the argument and a willingness to think hard about its various steps.

PART I
NATURAL ATHEOLOGY

a The Problem of Evil

Suppose we begin with what I have called natural atheology—the attempt to prove that God does not exist or that at any rate it is unreasonable or irrational to believe that He does. Perhaps the most widely accepted and impressive piece of natural atheology has to do with the so-called problem of evil. Many philosophers believe that the existence of evil constitutes a difficulty for the theist, and many believe that the existence of evil (or at least the amount and kinds of evil we actually find) makes belief in God unreasonable or rationally unacceptable.

The world does indeed contain a great deal of evil, some of which is catalogued by David Hume:

> But though these external insults, said Demea, from animals, from men, from all the elements, which assault us form a frightful catalogue of woes, they are nothing in comparison of those which arise within ourselves, from the distempered condition of our mind and body. How many lie under the lingering torment of diseases? Hear the pathetic enumeration of the great poet.
>
> > *Intestine stone and ulcer, colic-pangs,*
> > *Demoniac frenzy, moping melancholy,*
> > *And moon-struck madness, pining atrophy,*
> > *Marasmus, and wide-wasting pestilence.*
> > *Dire was the tossing, deep the groans:* Despair
> > *Tended the sick, busiest from couch to couch.*

> *And over them triumphant* Death *his dart*
> *Shook: but delay'd to strike, though oft invok'd*
> *With vows, as their chief good and final hope.*

The disorders of the mind, continued Demea, though more secret, are not perhaps less dismal and vexatious. Remorse, shame, anguish, rage, disappointment, anxiety, fear, dejection, despair—who has ever passed through life without cruel inroads from these tormentors? How many have scarcely ever felt any better sensations? Labor and poverty, so abhorred by everyone, are the certain lot of the far greater number; and those few privileged persons who enjoy ease and opulence never reach contentment or true felicity. All the goods of life united would not make a very happy man, but all the ills united would make a wretch indeed; and any one of them almost (and who can be free from every one), nay, often the absence of one good (and who can possess all) is sufficient to render life ineligible.[1]

In addition to "natural" evils such as earthquakes, tidal waves, and virulent diseases there are evils that result from human stupidity, arrogance, and cruelty. Some of these are described in painfully graphic detail in Dostoevski's *The Brothers Karamazov:*

"A Bulgarian I met lately in Moscow," Ivan went on, seeming not to hear his brother's words, "told me about the crimes committed by Turks and Circassians in all parts of Bulgaria through fear of a general rising of the Slavs. They burn villages, murder, outrage women and children, they nail their prisoners by the ears to the fences, leave them so till morning, and in the morning they hang them—all sorts of things you can't imagine. People talk sometimes of bestial cruelty, but that's a great injustice and insult to the beasts; a beast can never be so cruel as a man, so artistically cruel. The tiger only tears and gnaws, that's all he can do. He would never think of nailing people by the ears, even if he were able to do it. These Turks took a pleasure in torturing children, too; cutting the unborn child from the mother's womb, and tossing babies up in the air and catching them on the points of their bayonets before their mother's eyes. Doing it before the mother's eyes was what gave zest to the amusement. Here is

1. David Hume, *Dialogues Concerning Natural Religion*, ed. Nelson Pike (New York: Bobbs-Merrill Co., Inc., 1970), pt. X, pp. 84–85. The "great poet" referred to is John Milton, and the quotation is from *Paradise Lost*, bk. XI.

another scene that I thought very interesting. Imagine a trembling mother with her baby in her arms, a circle of invading Turks around her. They've planned a diversion; they pet the baby, laugh to make it laugh. They succeed, the baby laughs. At that moment a Turk points a pistol four inches from the baby's face. The baby laughs with glee, holds out his little hands to the pistol, and he pulls the trigger in the baby's face and blows out its brains. Artistic, wasn't it? By the way, Turks are particularly fond of sweet things, they say."[2]

There is also the suffering and savagery that go with war. Perhaps one of the worst features of war is the way in which it brutalizes those who take part in it. Commenting on the trial of Lt. William Calley, who was accused of taking part in the 1969 American massacre of unarmed civilians at My Lai, a young soldier said, "How can they punish Calley? They send us over here to kill dinks. Our job is to kill dinks. How can they punish him for that?" One who speaks in this way has indeed become brutish. Socrates once said that it is better to suffer injustice than to do it—better to be victim than perpetrator. Perhaps he's right; perhaps one who has become as morally callous and insensitive as that comment reveals has lost something more precious than life itself.

1. The Question: Why Does God Permit Evil?

So the world obviously contains a great deal of evil. Now the atheological discussion often begins with a question. If God is as benevolent as Christian theists claim, He must be just as appalled as we are at all this evil. But if He is also as powerful as they claim, then presumably He is in a position to do something about it. So why does He permit it? Why doesn't He arrange things so that these evils don't occur? That should have been easy enough for one as powerful as He. As Hume puts it:

2. Fyodor Dostoevski, *The Brothers Karamazov*, trans. Constance Garnett (New York: Random House, 1933), pp. 245–246.

Is he willing to prevent evil, but not able? Then he is impotent. Is he able, but not willing? Then he is malevolent. Is he both able and willing? Whence then is evil?

and

Why is there any misery at all in the world? Not by chance, surely. From some cause, then. It is from the intention of the deity? But he is perfectly benevolent. Is it contrary to his intention? But he is almighty. Nothing can shake the solidity of this reasoning, so short, so clear, so decisive. . . .[3]

So Hume insists on this question: if God is perfectly benevolent and also omnipotent, or almighty, why is there any evil in the world? Why does he permit it?

Now one reply would be to specify God's reason for permitting evil or for creating a world that contained evil. (Perhaps evil is necessary, in some way, to the existence of good.) Such an answer to Hume's question is sometimes called a *theodicy*. When a theist answers the question "Whence evil?" or "Why does God permit evil?" he is giving a theodicy. And, of course, a theist might like to have a theodicy, an answer to the question why God permits evil. He might want very badly to know why God permits evil in general or some particular evil—the death or suffering of someone close to him, or perhaps his own suffering. But suppose none of the suggested theodicies is very satisfactory. Or suppose that the theist admits he just doesn't know why God permits evil. What follows from that? Very little of interest. Why suppose that if God *does* have a good reason for permitting evil, the theist would be the first to know? Perhaps God has a good reason, but that reason is too complicated for us to understand. Or perhaps He has not revealed it for some other reason. The fact that the theist doesn't know why God permits evil is, perhaps, an interesting fact about the theist, but by itself it shows little or nothing relevant to the rationality of belief in God. Much more is needed for the atheological argument even to get off the ground.

3. Hume, *Dialogues Concerning Natural Religion*, pt. X, pp. 88, 91.

Perhaps we can see this as follows. The theist believes that God has a reason for permitting evil; he doesn't know what that reason is. But why should that mean that his belief is improper or irrational? Take an analogy. I believe that there is a connection of some sort between Paul's deciding to mow the lawn and the complex group of bodily movements involved in so doing. But *what* connection, exactly? Does his decision *cause* these bodily movements? If so, how? The decision may take place long before he so much as sets foot on the lawn. Is there an intermediary causal chain extending between the decision and the first of these movements? If so, what sorts of events make up this chain and how is the decision related, let's say, to the first event in it? Does it *have* a first event? And there are whole series of bodily motions involved in mowing the lawn. Is his decision related in the same way to each of these motions? Exactly what is the relation between his deciding to mow the lawn—which decision does not seem to be a bodily event at all—and his actually doing so? No one, I suspect, knows the answer to these questions. But does it follow that it is irrational or unreasonable to believe that this decision has something to do with that series of motions? Surely not. In the same way the theist's not knowing why God permits evil does not by itself show that he is irrational in thinking that God does indeed have a reason. To make out his case, therefore, the atheologian cannot rest content with asking embarrassing questions to which the theist does not know the answer. He must do more—he might try, for example, to show that it is *impossible* or anyhow unlikely that God should have a reason for permitting evil. Many philosophers—for example, some of the French Encyclopedists, J. S. Mill, F. H. Bradley, and many others—have claimed that there is a *contradiction* involved in asserting, as the theist does, that God is perfectly good, omnipotent (i.e., all-powerful), and omniscient (i.e., all-knowing) on the one hand, and, on the other, that there is evil.

2.   Does the Theist Contradict Himself?

In a widely discussed piece entitled "Evil and Omnipotence" John Mackie repeats this claim:

> I think, however, that a more telling criticism can be made by way of the traditional problem of evil. Here it can be shown, not that religious beliefs lack rational support, but that they are positively irrational, that the several parts of the essential theological doctrine are *inconsistent* with one another. . . .[4]

Is Mackie right? Does the theist contradict himself? But we must ask a prior question: just what is being claimed here? That theistic belief contains an inconsistency or contradiction, of course. But what, exactly, is an inconsistency or contradiction? There are several kinds. An *explicit* contradiction is a *proposition* of a certain sort—a conjunctive proposition, one conjunct of which is the denial or negation of the other conjunct. For example:

Paul is a good tennis player, and it's false that Paul is a good tennis player.

(People seldom assert explicit contradictions). Is Mackie charging the theist with accepting such a contradiction? Presumably not; what he says is:

> In its simplest form the problem is this: God is omnipotent; God is wholly good; yet evil exists. There seems to be some contradiction between these three propositions, so that if any two of them were true the third would be false. But at the same time all three are essential parts of most theological positions; the theologian, it seems, at once *must* adhere and *cannot consistently* adhere to all three.[5]

According to Mackie, then, the theist accepts a group or set of three propositions; this set is inconsistent. Its members, of course, are

4. John Mackie, "Evil and Omnipotence," in *The Philosophy of Religion*, ed. Basil Mitchell (London: Oxford University Press, 1971), p. 92.
5. Ibid., pp. 92–93.

(1) God is omnipotent

(2) God is wholly good

and

(3) Evil exists.

Call this set A; the claim is that A is an inconsistent set. But what is it for a *set* to be inconsistent or contradictory? Following our definition of an explicit contradiction, we might say that a set of propositions is explicitly contradictory if one of the members is the denial or negation of another member. But then, of course, it is evident that the set we are discussing is not explicitly contradictory; the denials of (1), (2), and (3), respectively are

(1') God is not omnipotent (or it's false that God is omnipotent)

(2') God is not wholly good

and

(3') There is no evil

none of which are in set A.

Of course many sets are pretty clearly contradictory, in an important way, but not *explicitly* contradictory. For example, set B:

(4) If all men are mortal, then Socrates is mortal

(5) All men are mortal

(6) Socrates is not mortal.

This set is not explicitly contradictory; yet surely *some* significant sense of that term applies to it. What is important here is that by using only the rules of ordinary logic—the laws of propositional logic and quantification theory found in any introductory text on the subject—we can deduce an explicit contradiction from the set. Or to put it differently, we can use the laws of logic to deduce a proposition from the set, which proposition, when added to the set, yields a new set that is explicitly contradictory. For by using the law *modus ponens* (if p, then q; p; therefore q) we can deduce

(7) Socrates is mortal

from (4) and (5). The result of adding (7) to B is the set $\{(4), (5), (6), (7)\}$. This set, of course, is explicitly contradictory in that (6) is the denial of (7). We might say that any set which shares this characteristic with set B is *formally* contradictory. So a formally contradictory set is one from whose members an explicit contradiction can be deduced by the laws of logic. Is Mackie claiming that set A is formally contradictory?

If he is, he's wrong. No laws of logic permit us to deduce the denial of one of the propositions in A from the other members. Set A isn't formally contradictory either.

But there is still another way in which a set of propositions can be contradictory or inconsistent. Consider set C, whose members are

(8) George is older than Paul
(9) Paul is older than Nick

and

(10) George is not older than Nick.

This set is neither explicitly nor formally contradictory; we can't, just by using the laws of logic, deduce the denial of any of these propositions from the others. And yet there is a good sense in which it is inconsistent or contradictory. For clearly it is *not possible* that its three members all be true. It is *necessarily true* that

(11) If George is older than Paul, and Paul is older than Nick, then George is older than Nick.

And if we add (11) to set C, we get a set that is formally contradictory; (8), (9), and (11) yield, by the laws of ordinary logic, the denial of (10).

I said that (11) is *necessarily true;* but what does *that* mean? Of course we might say that a proposition is necessarily true if it is impossible that it be false, or if its negation is not possibly true. This would be to explain necessity in terms of possibility. Chances are, however, that anyone who does not know what necessity is, will be equally at a loss about possibility; the explanation is not likely to be very successful. Perhaps all we can do by way of explanation is give some examples and hope for the best. In the first place many propositions can be established by the laws of logic alone—for example

(12) If all men are mortal and Socrates is a man, then Socrates is mortal.

Such propositions are truths of logic; and all of them are necessary in the sense of question. But truths of arithmetic and mathematics generally are also necessarily true. Still further, there is a host of propositions that are neither truths of logic nor truths of mathematics but are nonetheless necessarily true; (11) would be an example, as well as

(13) Nobody is taller than himself
(14) Red is a color
(15) No numbers are persons
(16) No prime number is a prime minister

and

(17) Bachelors are unmarried.

So here we have an important kind of necessity—let's call it "broadly logical necessity." Of course there is a correlative kind of *possibility:* a proposition *p* is possibly true (in the broadly logical sense) just in case its negation or denial is not necessarily true (in that same broadly logical sense). This sense of necessity and possibility must be distinguished from another that we may call *causal* or *natural* necessity and possibility. Consider

(18) Henry Kissinger has swum the Atlantic.

Although this proposition has an implausible ring, it is not necessarily false in the broadly logical sense (and its denial is not necessarily true in that sense). But there is a good sense in which it is impossible: it is *causally* or *naturally* impossible. Human beings, unlike dolphins, just don't have the physical equipment demanded for this feat. Unlike Superman, furthermore, the rest of us are incapable of leaping tall buildings at a single bound or (without auxiliary power of some kind) traveling faster than a speeding bullet. These things are *impossible* for us—but not *logically* impossible, even in the broad sense.

So there are several senses of necessity and possibility here. There are a number of propositions, furthermore, of which it's difficult to say whether they are or aren't possible in the broadly logical sense; some of these are subjects of philosophical controversy. Is it possible, for example, for a person never to be conscious during his entire existence? Is it possible for a (human) person to exist *disembodied?* If that's possible, is it possible that there be a person who *at no time at all* during his entire existence has a body? Is it possible to see without eyes? These are propositions about whose possibility in that broadly logical sense there is disagreement and dispute.

Now return to set C (p. 14). What is characteristic of it is the fact that the conjunction of its members—the proposition expressed by the result of putting "and's" between (8), (9), and (10)—is necessarily false. Or we might put it like this: what characterizes set C is the fact that we can get a formally contradictory set by adding a necessarily true proposition—namely (11). Suppose we say that a set is *implicitly contradictory* if it resembles C in this respect. That is, a set S of propositions is implicitly contradictory if there is a necessary proposition *p* such that the result of adding *p* to S is a formally contradictory set. Another way to put it: S is implicitly contradictory if there is some necessarily true proposition *p* such that by using just the laws of ordinary logic, we can deduce an explicit contradiction from *p* together with the members of S. And when Mackie says that set A is contradictory, we may properly take him, I think, as holding that it is implicitly contradictory in the explained sense. As he puts it:

> However, the contradiction does not arise immediately; to show it we need some additional premises, or perhaps some quasi-logical rules connecting the terms "good" and "evil" and "omnipotent." These additional principles are that good is opposed to evil, in such a way that a good thing always eliminates evil as far as it can, and that there are no limits to what an omnipotent thing can do. From these it follows that a good omnipotent thing eliminates evil completely, and then the propositions that a good omnipotent thing exists, and that evil exists, are incompatible.[6]

Here Mackie refers to "additional premises"; he also calls them "additional principles" and "quasi-logical rules"; he says we need them to

6. Ibid., p. 93.

show the contradiction. What he means, I think, is that to get a formally contradictory set we must add some more propositions to set A; and if we aim to show that set A is implicitly contradictory, these propositions must be necessary truths—"quasi-logical rules" as Mackie calls them. The two additional principles he suggests are

(19) A good thing always eliminates evil as far as it can

and

(20) There are no limits to what an omnipotent being can do.

And, of course, if Mackie means to show that set A is implicitly contradictory, then he must hold that (19) and (20) are not merely *true* but *necessarily true*.

But, are they? What about (20) first? What does it mean to say that a being is omnipotent? That he is *all-powerful*, or *almighty*, presumably. But are there no limits *at all* to the power of such a being? Could he create square circles, for example, or married bachelors? Most theologians and theistic philosophers who hold that God is omnipotent, do not hold that He can create round squares or bring it about that He both exists and does not exist. These theologians and philosophers may hold that there are no *nonlogical* limits to what an omnipotent being can do, but they concede that not even an omnipotent being can bring about logically impossible states of affairs or cause necessarily false propositions to be true. Some theists, on the other hand—Martin Luther and Descartes, perhaps—have apparently thought that God's power is unlimited even by the laws of logic. For these theists the question whether set A is contradictory will not be of much interest. As theists they believe (1) and (2), and they also, presumably, believe (3). But they remain undisturbed by the claim that (1), (2), and (3) are jointly inconsistent—because, as they say, God can do what is logically impossible. Hence He can bring it about that the members of set A are all true, even if that set is contradictory (concentrating very intensely upon this suggestion is likely to make you dizzy). So the theist who thinks that the power of God isn't limited *at all*, not even by the laws of logic, will be unimpressed by Mackie's argument and won't find any difficulty in the contradiction set A is alleged to contain. This view is not very popular, however, and for good reason; it is quite incoherent. What the theist typically means when he says that God is omnipotent is not that there are *no* limits to God's power, but at most that there are no nonlogical limits to what He can do; and given this qualification, it is perhaps initially plausible to suppose that (20) is necessarily true.

But what about (19), the proposition that every good thing eliminates every evil state of affairs that it can eliminate? Is that necessarily true? Is it true at all? Suppose, first of all, that your friend Paul unwisely goes for a drive on a wintry day and runs out of gas on a deserted road. The temperature dips to $-10°$, and a miserably cold wind comes up. You are sitting comfortably at home (twenty-five miles from Paul) roasting chestnuts in a roaring blaze. Your car is in the garage; in the trunk there is the full five-gallon can of gasoline you always keep for emergencies. Paul's discomfort and danger are certainly an evil, and one which you could eliminate. You don't do so. But presumably you don't thereby forfeit your claim to being a "good thing"—you simply didn't know of Paul's plight. And so (19) does not appear to be necessary. It says that every good thing has a certain property—the property of eliminating every evil that it can. And if the case I described is possible—a good person's failing through ignorance to eliminate a certain evil he can eliminate—then (19) is by no means necessarily true.

But perhaps Mackie could sensibly claim that if you *didn't know* about Paul's plight, then in fact you were *not*, at the time in question, able to eliminate the evil in question; and perhaps he'd be right. In any event he could revise (19) to take into account the kind of case I mentioned:

(19a) Every good thing always eliminates every evil that *it knows about* and can eliminate.

{(1), (2), (3), (20), (19a)}, you'll notice, is not a formally contradictory set—to get a formal contradiction we must add a proposition specifying that God *knows about* every evil state of affairs. But most theists do believe that God is omniscient or all-knowing; so if this new set—the set that results when we add to set A the proposition that God is omniscient—is implicitly contradictory then Mackie should be satisfied and the theist confounded. (And, henceforth, set A will be the old set A together with the proposition that God is omniscient.)

But is (19a) necessary? Hardly. Suppose you know that Paul is marooned as in the previous example, and you also know another friend is similarly marooned fifty miles in the opposite direction. Suppose, furthermore, that while you can rescue one or the other, you simply can't rescue both. Then each of the two evils is such that it is within your power to eliminate it; and you know about them both. But you can't eliminate *both;* and you don't forfeit your claim to being a good person by eliminating only one—it wasn't within your power to do more. So the fact that you don't doesn't mean that you are not a good person. Therefore (19a) is false; it is not a necessary truth or even a truth that every good thing eliminates every evil it knows about and can eliminate.

We can see the same thing another way. You've been rock climbing. Still something of a novice, you've acquired a few cuts and bruises by inelegantly using your knees rather than your feet. One of these bruises is fairly painful. You mention it to a physician friend, who predicts the pain will leave of its own accord in a day or two. Meanwhile, he says, there's nothing he can do, short of amputating your leg above the knee, to remove the pain. Now the pain in your knee is an evil state of affairs. All else being equal, it would be better if you had no such pain. And it is within the power of your friend to eliminate this evil state of affairs. Does his failure to do so mean that he is not a good person? Of course not; for he could eliminate this evil state of affairs only by bringing about another, much worse evil. And so it is once again evident that (19a) is false. It is entirely possible that a good person fail to eliminate an evil state of affairs that he knows about and can eliminate. This would take place, if, as in the present example, he couldn't eliminate the evil without bringing about a *greater* evil.

A slightly different kind of case shows the same thing. A really impressive good state of affairs G will *outweigh* a trivial evil E—that is, the

conjunctive state of affairs G *and* E is itself a good state of affairs. And
surely a good person would not be obligated to eliminate a given evil if
he could do so only by eliminating a good that outweighed it. Therefore
(19a) is not necessarily true; it can't be used to show that set A is
implicitly contradictory.

These difficulties might suggest another revision of (19); we might try

> (19b) A good being eliminates every evil E that it knows about and that
> it can eliminate without either bringing about a greater evil or eliminat-
> ing a good state of affairs that outweighs E.

Is this necessarily true? It takes care of the second of the two difficulties afflicting (19a) but leaves the first untouched. We can see this as
follows. First, suppose we say that a being *properly eliminates* an evil
state of affairs if it eliminates that evil without either eliminating an
outweighing good or bringing about a greater evil. It is then obviously
possible that a person find himself in a situation where he could properly
eliminate an evil E and could also properly eliminate another evil E',
but couldn't properly eliminate them *both*. You're rock climbing again,
this time on the dreaded north face of the Grand Teton. You and your
party come upon Curt and Bob, two mountaineers stranded 125 feet
apart on the face. They untied to reach their cigarettes and then care-
lessly dropped the rope while lighting up. A violent, dangerous thunderstorm is approaching. You have time to rescue one of the stranded
climbers and retreat before the storm hits; if you rescue both, however,
you and your party and the two climbers will be caught on the face
during the thunderstorm, which will very likely destroy your entire party.
In this case you can eliminate one evil (Curt's being stranded on the
face) without causing more evil or eliminating a greater good; and you
are also able to properly eliminate the other evil (Bob's being thus
stranded). But you can't properly eliminate them *both*. And so the fact
that you don't rescue Curt, say, even though you could have, doesn't
show that you aren't a good person. Here, then, each of the evils is such
that you can properly eliminate it; but you can't properly eliminate them
both, and hence can't be blamed for failing to eliminate one of them.

So neither (19a) nor (19b) is necessarily true. You may be tempted to reply that the sort of counterexamples offered—examples where someone is able to eliminate an evil A and also able to eliminate a different evil B, but unable to eliminate them both—are irrelevant to the case of a being who, like God, is both omnipotent and omniscient. That is, you may think that if an omnipotent and omniscient being is able to eliminate *each* of two evils, it follows that he can eliminate them *both*. Perhaps this is so; but it is not strictly to the point. The fact is the counterexamples show that (19a) and (19b) are not necessarily true and hence can't be used to show that set A is implicitly inconsistent. What the reply does suggest is that perhaps the atheologian will have more success if he works the properties of omniscience and omnipotence into (19). Perhaps he could say something like

(19c) An omnipotent and omniscient good being eliminates every evil that it can properly eliminate.

And suppose, for purposes of argument, we concede the necessary truth of (19c). Will it serve Mackie's purposes? Not obviously. For we don't get a set that is formally contradictory by adding (20) and (19c) to set A. This set (call it A') contains the following six members:

(1) God is omnipotent
(2) God is wholly good
(2') God is omniscient
(3) Evil exists
(19c) An omnipotent and omniscient good being eliminates every evil that it can properly eliminate

and

(20) There are no nonlogical limits to what an omnipotent being can do.

Now if A' were formally contradictory, then from any five of its members we could deduce the denial of the sixth by the laws of ordinary logic. That is, any five would *formally entail* the denial of the sixth. So if A' were formally inconsistent, the denial of (3) would be formally entailed by the remaining five. That is, (1), (2), (2'), (19c), and (20) would formally entail

(3') There is no evil.

But they don't; what they formally entail is not that there is no evil *at all* but only that

(3") There is no evil that God can properly eliminate.

So (19c) doesn't really help either—not because it is not necessarily true but because its addition [with (20)] to set A does not yield a formally contradictory set.

Obviously, what the atheologian must add to get a formally contradictory set is

(21) If God is omniscient and omnipotent, then he can properly eliminate every evil state of affairs.

Suppose we agree that the set consisting in A plus (19c), (20), and (21) is formally contradictory. So if (19c), (20), and (21) are all necessarily true, then set A is implicitly contradictory. We've already conceded that (19c) and (20) are indeed necessary. So we must take a look at (21). Is this proposition necessarily true?

No. To see this let us ask the following question. Under what conditions would an omnipotent being be unable to eliminate a certain evil E without eliminating an outweighing good? Well, suppose that E is *included in* some good state of affairs that outweighs it. That is, suppose there is some good state of affairs G so related to E that it is impossible that G obtain or be actual and E fail to obtain. (Another way to put this: a state of affairs S includes S' if the conjunctive state of affairs S *but not S'* is impossible, or if it is necessary that S' obtains if S does.) Now suppose that some good state of affairs G includes an evil state of affairs E that it outweighs. Then not even an omnipotent being could eliminate E without eliminating G. But *are* there any cases where a good state of affairs includes, in this sense, an evil that it outweighs?[7] Indeed there are such states of affairs. To take an artificial example, let's

---

[7]More simply, the question is really just whether any good state of affairs includes an evil; a little reflection reveals that no good state of affairs can include an evil that it does *not* outweigh.

suppose that E is Paul's suffering from a minor abrasion and G is your being deliriously happy. The conjunctive state of affairs, G and E—the state of affairs that obtains if and only if both G and E obtain—is then a good state of affairs: it is better, all else being equal, that you be intensely happy and Paul suffer a mildly annoying abrasion than that this state of affairs not obtain. So G and E is a good state of affairs. And clearly G and E includes E: obviously it is necessarily true that if you are deliriously happy and Paul is suffering from an abrasion, then Paul is suffering from an abrasion.

But perhaps you think this example trivial, tricky, slippery, and irrelevant. If so, take heart; other examples abound. Certain kinds of values, certain familiar kinds of good states of affairs, can't exist apart from evil of some sort. For example, there are people who display a sort of creative moral heroism in the face of suffering and adversity—a heroism that inspires others and creates a good situation out of a bad one. In a situation like this the evil, of course, remains evil; but the total state of affairs—someone's bearing pain magnificently, for example—may be good. If it is, then the good present must outweigh the evil; otherwise the total situation would not be good. But, of course, it is not possible that such a good state of affairs obtain unless some evil also obtain. It is a necessary truth that if someone bears pain magnificently, then someone is in pain.

The conclusion to be drawn, therefore, is that (21) is not necessarily true. And our discussion thus far shows at the very least that it is no easy matter to find necessarily true propositions that yield a formally contradictory set when added to set A.[8] One wonders, therefore, why the many atheologians who confidently assert that this set is contradictory make no attempt whatever to *show* that it is. For the most part they are content just to *assert* that there is a contradiction here. Even Mackie, who sees that some "additional premises" or "quasi-logical rules" are needed, makes scarcely a beginning towards finding some additional

8. In Plantinga, *God and Other Minds* (Ithaca, N.Y.: Cornell University Press, 1967), chap. 5, I explore further the project of finding such propositions.

premises that are necessarily true and that together with the members of set A formally entail an explicit contradiction.

3. Can We Show That There Is No Inconsistency Here?

To summarize our conclusions so far: although many atheologians claim that the theist is involved in contradiction when he asserts the members of set A, this set, obviously, is neither *explicitly* nor *formally* contradictory; the claim, presumably, must be that it is *implicitly* contradictory. To make good this claim the atheologian must find some necessarily true proposition *p* (it could be a conjunction of several propositions) such that the addition of *p* to set A yields a set that is formally contradictory. No atheologian has produced even a plausible candidate for this role, and it certainly is not easy to see what such a proposition might be. Now we might think we should simply declare set A implicitly consistent on the principle that a proposition (or set) is to be presumed consistent or possible until proven otherwise. This course, however, leads to trouble. The same principle would impel us to declare the atheologian's claim—that set A is *inconsistent*—possible or consistent. But the claim that a given set of propositions is implicitly contradictory, is itself either necessarily true or necessarily false; so if such a claim is *possible,* it is not necessarily false and is, therefore, true (in fact, necessarily true). If we followed the suggested principle, therefore, we should be obliged to declare set A implicitly consistent (since it hasn't been shown to be otherwise), but we should have to say the same thing about the atheologian's claim, since we haven't shown *that* claim to be inconsistent or impossible. The atheologian's claim, furthermore, is necessarily true if it is possible. Accordingly, if we accept the above principle, we shall have to declare set A both implicitly consistent and implicitly inconsistent. So all we can say at this point is that set A has not been shown to be implicitly inconsistent.

Can we go any further? One way to go on would be to try to *show* that set A is implicitly consistent or possible in the broadly logical sense. But what is involved in showing such a thing? Although there are various ways to approach this matter, they all resemble one another in an important respect. They all amount to this: to show that a set *S* is consistent you think of a *possible state of affairs* (it needn't *actually obtain*) which is such that if it were actual, then all of the members of *S* would be true. This procedure is sometimes called *giving a model of S*. For example, you might construct an axiom set and then show that it is consistent by giving a model of it; this is how it was shown that the denial of Euclid's parallel postulate is formally consistent with the rest of his postulates.

There are various special cases of this procedure to fit special circumstances. Suppose, for example, you have a pair of propositions *p* and *q* and wish to show them consistent. And suppose we say that a proposition p_1 *entails* a proposition p_2 if it is impossible that p_1 be true and p_2 false—if the conjunctive proposition p_1 *and not* p_2 is necessarily false. Then one way to show that *p* is consistent with *q* is to find some proposition *r* whose conjunction with *p* is both possible, in the broadly logical sense, and entails *q*. A rude and unlettered behaviorist, for example, might hold that thinking is really nothing but movements of the larynx; he might go on to hold that

P Jones did not move his larynx after April 30

is inconsistent (in the broadly logical sense) with

Q Jones did some thinking during May

By way of rebuttal, we might point out that *P* appears to be consistent with

R While convalescing from an April 30 laryngotomy, Jones whiled away the idle hours by writing (in May) a splendid paper on Kant's *Critique of Pure Reason.*

So the conjunction of *P* and *R* appears to be consistent; but obviously it also entails *Q* (you can't write even a passable paper on Kant's *Critique of Pure Reason* without doing some thinking); so *P* and *Q* are consistent.

We can see that this is a special case of the procedure I mentioned above as follows. This proposition *R* is consistent with *P*; so the proposition *P and R* is possible, describes a possible state of affairs. But *P and R* entails *Q*; hence if *P and R* were true, *Q* would also be true, and hence both *P* and *Q* would be true. So this is really a case of producing a possible state of affairs such that, if it were actual, all the members of the set in question (in this case the pair set of *P* and *Q*) would be true.

How does this apply to the case before us? As follows. Let us conjoin propositions (1), (2), and (2') and henceforth call the result (1):

(1) God is omniscient, omnipotent, and wholly good

The problem, then, is to show that (1) and (3) (evil exists) are consistent. This could be done, as we've seen, by finding a proposition *r* that is consistent with (1) and such that (1) and (*r*) together entail (3). One proposition that might do the trick is

(22) God creates a world containing evil and has a good reason for doing so.

If (22) is consistent with (1), then it follows that (1) and (3) (and hence set A) are consistent. Accordingly, one thing some theists have tried is to show that (22) and (1) are consistent.

One can attempt this in at least two ways. On the one hand, we could try to apply the same method again. Conceive of a possible state of affairs such that, if it obtained, an omnipotent, omniscient, and wholly good God would have a good reason for permitting evil. On the other, someone might try to specify *what God's reason is* for permitting evil and try to show, if it is not obvious, that it is a good reason. St. Augustine, for example, one of the greatest and most influential philosopher-theologians of the Christian Church, writes as follows:

> . . . some people see with perfect truth that a creature is better if, while possessing free will, it remains always fixed upon God and never sins; then, reflecting on men's sins, they are grieved, not because they continue to sin, but because they were created. They say: He should have made us such that

we never willed to sin, but always to enjoy the unchangeable truth.

They should not lament or be angry. God has not compelled men to sin just because He created them and gave them the power to choose between sinning and not sinning. There are angels who have never sinned and never will sin.

Such is the generosity of God's goodness that He has not refrained from creating even that creature which He foreknew would not only sin, but remain in the will to sin. As a runaway horse is better than a stone which does not run away because it lacks self-movement and sense perception, so the creature is more excellent which sins by free will than that which does not sin only because it has no free will.[9]

In broadest terms Augustine claims that God could create a better, more perfect universe by permitting evil than He could by refusing to do so:

Neither the sins nor the misery are necessary to the perfection of the universe, but souls as such are necessary, which have the power to sin if they so will, and become miserable if they sin. If misery persisted after their sins had been abolished, or if there were misery before there were sins, then it might be right to say that the order and government of the universe were at fault. Again, if there were sins but no consequent misery, that order is equally dishonored by lack of equity.[10]

Augustine tries to tell us *what God's reason is* for permitting evil. At bottom, he says, it's that God can create a more perfect universe by permitting evil. A really top-notch universe requires the existence of free, rational, and moral agents; and some of the free creatures He created went wrong. But the universe with the free creatures it contains and the evil they commit is better than it would have been had it contained neither the free creatures nor this evil. Such an attempt to specify God's reason for permitting evil is what I earlier called a *theodicy;* in the words of John Milton it is an attempt to "justify the ways of God to man," to show that God is just in·permitting evil. Augustine's kind of theodicy might be called a Free Will Theodicy, since the idea of rational creatures with free will plays such a prominent role in it.

9. *The Problem of Free Choice*, Vol. 22 of *Ancient Christian Writers* (Westminster, Md.: The Newman Press, 1955), bk. 2, pp. 14–15.

10. Ibid., bk. 3, p. 9.

A theodicist, then, attempts to tell us why God permits evil. Quite distinct from a Free Will Theodicy is what I shall call a Free Will Defense. Here the aim is not to say what God's reason *is*, but at most what God's reason *might possibly be*. We could put the difference like this. The Free Will Theodicist and Free Will Defender are both trying to show that (1) is consistent with (22), and of course if so, then set A is consistent. The Free Will Theodicist tries to do this by finding some proposition *r* which in conjunction with (1) entails (22); he claims, furthermore, that this proposition is *true*, not just consistent with (1). He tries to tell us what God's reason for permitting evil *really is*. The Free Will Defender, on the other hand, though he also tries to find a proposition *r* that is consistent with (1) and in conjunction with it entails (22), does *not* claim to know or even believe that *r* is true. And here, of course, he is perfectly within his rights. His aim is to show that (1) is consistent with (22); all he need do then is find an *r* that is consistent with (1) and such that (1) and *(r)* entail (22); whether *r* is *true* is quite beside the point.

So there is a significant difference between a Free Will Theodicy and a Free Will Defense. The latter is sufficient (if successful) to show that set A is consistent; in a way a Free Will Theodicy goes beyond what is required. On the other hand, a theodicy would be much more satisfying, if possible to achieve. No doubt the theist would rather know what God's reason *is* for permitting evil than simply that it's possible that He has a good one. But in the present context (that of investigating the consistency of set A), the latter is all that's needed. Neither a defense or a theodicy, of course, gives any hint as to what God's reason for some *specific* evil—the death or suffering of someone close to you, for example —might be. And there is still another function—a sort of pastoral function[11]—in the neighborhood that neither serves. Confronted with evil in his own life or suddenly coming to realize more clearly than before the *extent* and *magnitude* of evil, a believer in God may undergo a crisis

11. I am indebted to Henry Schuurman (in conversation) for helpful discussion of the difference between this pastoral function and those served by a theodicy or a defense.

of faith. He may be tempted to follow the advice of Job's "friends"; he may be tempted to "curse God and die." Neither a Free Will Defense nor a Free Will Theodicy is designed to be of much help or comfort to one suffering from such a storm in the soul (although in a specific case, of course, one or the other could prove useful). Neither is to be thought of first of all as a means of pastoral counseling. Probably neither will enable someone to find peace with himself and with God in the face of the evil the world contains. But then, of course, neither is intended for that purpose.

4. The Free Will Defense

In what follows I shall focus attention upon the Free Will Defense. I shall examine it more closely, state it more exactly, and consider objections to it; and I shall argue that in the end it is successful. Earlier we saw that among good states of affairs there are some that not even God can bring about without bringing about evil: those goods, namely, that *entail* or *include* evil states of affairs. The Free Will Defense can be looked upon as an effort to show that there may be a very different kind of good that God can't bring about without permitting evil. These are good states of affairs that don't include evil; they do not entail the existence of any evil whatever; nonetheless God Himself can't bring them about without permitting evil.

So how does the Free Will Defense work? And what does the Free Will Defender mean when he says that people are or may be free? What is relevant to the Free Will Defense is the idea of *being free with respect to an action*. If a person is free with respect to a given action, then he is free to perform that action and free to refrain from performing it; no antecedent conditions and/or causal laws determine that he will perform the action, or that he won't. It is within his power, at the time in question, to take or perform the action and within his power to refrain from it. Freedom so conceived is not to be confused with unpredictability. You might be able to predict what you will do in a given situation even if you are free, in that situation, to do something else. If I know you well, I may be able to predict what action you will take in response to a certain set of conditions; it does not follow that you are not free with respect to that action. Secondly, I shall say that an action is *morally significant*, for a given person, if it would be wrong for him to perform the action but right to refrain or *vice versa*. Keeping a promise, for example, would ordinarily be morally significant for a person, as would refusing induction into the army. On the other hand, having Cheerios for breakfast (instead of Wheaties) would not normally be morally significant. Further, suppose we say that a person is *significantly free*, on a given occasion, if he is then free with respect to a morally significant action. And finally we must distinguish between *moral evil* and *natural evil*. The former is evil that results from free human activity; natural evil is any other kind of evil.[12]

Given these definitions and distinctions, we can make a preliminary statement of the Free Will Defense as follows. A world containing creatures who are significantly free (and freely perform more good than evil actions) is more valuable, all else being equal, than a world containing no free creatures at all. Now God can create free creatures, but He can't *cause* or *determine* them to do only what is right. For if He does so, then they aren't significantly free after all; they do not do what is right *freely*. To create creatures capable of *moral good*, therefore, He must create creatures capable of moral evil; and He can't give these creatures the freedom to perform evil and at the same time prevent them from doing so. As it turned out, sadly enough, some of the free creatures God created went wrong in the exercise of their freedom; this is the source of moral evil. The fact that free creatures sometimes go wrong, however, counts neither against God's omnipotence nor against His goodness; for He could have forestalled the occurrence of moral evil only by removing the possibility of moral good.

12. This distinction is not very precise (how, exactly, are we to construe "results from"?); but perhaps it will serve our present purposes.

I said earlier that the Free Will Defender tries to find a proposition that is consistent with

(1) God is omniscient, omnipotent, and wholly good

and together with (1) entails that there is evil. According to the Free Will Defense, we must find this proposition somewhere in the above story. The heart of the Free Will Defense is the claim that it is *possible* that God could not have created a universe containing moral good (or as much moral good as this world contains) without creating one that also contained moral evil. And if so, then it is possible that God has a good reason for creating a world containing evil.

Now this defense has met with several kinds of objections. For example, some philosophers say that *causal determinism* and *freedom*, contrary to what we might have thought, are not really incompatible.[13] But if so, then God could have created free creatures who were free, and free to do what is wrong, but nevertheless were causally determined to do only what is right. Thus He could have created creatures who were free to do what was wrong, while nevertheless preventing them from ever performing any wrong actions—simply by seeing to it that they were causally determined to do only what is right. Of course this contradicts the Free Will Defense, according to which there is inconsistency in supposing that God determines free creatures to do only what is right. But is it really possible that all of a person's actions are causally determined while some of them are free? How could that be so? According to one version of the doctrine in question, to say that George acts freely on a given occasion is to say only this: *if George had chosen to do otherwise, he would have done otherwise.* Now George's action *A* is causally determined if some event *E*—some event beyond his control —has already occurred, where the state of affairs consisting in *E*'s occurrence conjoined with George's *refraining* from performing *A*, is a causally impossible state of affairs. Then one can consistently hold both

13. See, for example, A. Flew, "Divine Omnipotence and Human Freedom," in *New Essays in Philosophical Theology*, eds. A. Flew and A. MacIntyre (London: SCM, 1955), pp. 150–153.

that all of a man's actions are causally determined and that some of them are free in the above sense. For suppose that all of a man's actions are causally determined and that he *couldn't*, on any occasion, have made any choice or performed any action different from the ones he did make and perform. It could still be true that if he *had* chosen to do otherwise, he would have done otherwise. Granted, he couldn't have chosen to do otherwise; but this is consistent with saying that *if* he had, things would have gone differently.

This objection to the Free Will Defense seems utterly implausible. One might as well claim that being in jail doesn't really limit one's freedom on the grounds that if one were *not* in jail, he'd be free to come and go as he pleased. So I shall say no more about this objection here.[14]

A second objection is more formidable. In essence it goes like this. Surely it is possible to do only what is right, even if one is free to do wrong. It is *possible*, in that broadly logical sense, that there be a world containing free creatures who always do what is right. There is certainly no *contradiction* or *inconsistency* in this idea. But God is omnipotent; his power has no nonlogical limitations. So if it's possible that there be a world containing creatures who are free to do what is wrong but never in fact do so, then it follows that an omnipotent God could create such a world. If so, however, the Free Will Defense must be mistaken in its insistence upon the possibility that God is omnipotent but unable to create a world containing moral good without permitting moral evil. J. L. Mackie (above, p. 12) states this objection:

> If God has made men such that in their free choices they sometimes prefer what is good and sometimes what is evil, why could he not have made men such that they always freely choose the good? If there is no logical impossibility in a man's freely choosing the good on one, or on several occasions, there cannot be a logical impossibility in his freely choosing the good on every occasion. God was not, then, faced with a choice between making innocent automata and making beings who, in acting freely, would sometimes go wrong; there was open to him the obviously better possibility of making beings who would act freely but always go right. Clearly, his failure

14. For further discussion of it see Plantinga, *God and Other Minds*, pp. 132–135.

to avail himself of this possibility is inconsistent with his being both omnipotent and wholly good.[15]

Now what, exactly, is Mackie's point here? This. According to the Free Will Defense, it is possible both that God is omnipotent and that He was unable to create a world containing moral good without creating one containing moral evil. But, replies Mackie, this limitation on His power to create is inconsistent with God's omnipotence. For surely it's *possible* that there be a world containing perfectly virtuous persons— persons who are significantly free but always do what is right. Surely there are *possible worlds* that contain moral good but no moral evil. But God, if He is omnipotent, can create any possible world He chooses. So it is *not* possible, contrary to the Free Will Defense, both that God is omnipotent and that He could create a world containing moral good only by creating one containing moral evil. If He is omnipotent, the only limitations of His power are *logical* limitations; in which case there are no possible worlds He could not have created.

This is a subtle and important point. According to the great German philosopher G.W. Leibniz, *this* world, the actual world, must be the best of all possible worlds. His reasoning goes as follows. Before God created anything at all, He was confronted with an enormous range of choices; He could create or bring into actuality any of the myriads of different possible worlds. Being perfectly good, He must have chosen to create the best world He could; being omnipotent, He was able to create any possible world He pleased. He must, therefore, have chosen the best of all possible worlds; and hence *this* world, the one He did create, must be the best possible. Now Mackie, of course, agrees with Leibniz that God, if omnipotent, could have created any world He pleased and would have created the best world he could. But while Leibniz draws the conclusion that this world, despite appearances, must be the best possible, Mackie concludes instead that there is no omnipotent, wholly good God. For, he says, it is obvious enough that this present world is not the best of all possible worlds.

15. Mackie, in *The Philosophy of Religion*, pp. 100–101.

The Free Will Defender disagrees with both Leibniz and Mackie. In the first place, he might say, what is the reason for supposing that *there is* such a thing as the best of all possible worlds? No matter how marvelous a world is—containing no matter how many persons enjoying unalloyed bliss—isn't it possible that there be an even better world containing even more persons enjoying even more unalloyed bliss? But what is really characteristic and central to the Free Will Defense is the claim that God, though omnipotent, could not have actualized just any possible world He pleased.

5. Was It within God's Power to Create Any Possible World He Pleased?

This is indeed the crucial question for the Free Will Defense. If we wish to discuss it with insight and authority, we shall have to look into the idea of *possible worlds*. And a sensible first question is this: what sort of thing is a possible world? The basic idea is that a possible world is a *way things could have been;* it is a *state of affairs* of some kind. Earlier we spoke of states of affairs, in particular of good and evil states of affairs. Suppose we look at this idea in more detail. What sort of thing is a state of affairs? The following would be examples:

> **Nixon's having won the 1972 election**
> **7 + 5's being equal to 12**
> **All men's being mortal**

and

> **Gary, Indiana's, having a really nasty pollution problem.**

These are *actual* states of affairs: states of affairs that do in fact *obtain*. And corresponding to each such actual state of affairs there is a true proposition—in the above cases, the corresponding propositions would be *Nixon won the 1972 presidential election, 7 + 5 is equal to 12, all men are mortal,* and *Gary, Indiana, has a really nasty pollution problem.*

A proposition *p* *corresponds* to a state of affairs *s*, in this sense, if it is impossible that *p* be true and *s* fail to obtain and impossible that *s* obtain and *p* fail to be true.

But just as there are false propositions, so there are states of affairs that do *not* obtain or are *not* actual. *Kissinger's having swum the Atlantic* and *Hubert Horatio Humphrey's having run a mile in four minutes* would be examples. Some states of affairs that do not obtain are *impossible:* e.g., *Hubert's having drawn a square circle, 7 + 5's being equal to 75,* and *Agnew's having a brother who was an only child.* The propositions corresponding to these states of affairs, of course, are necessarily false. So there are states of affairs that *obtain* or *are actual* and also states of affairs that don't obtain. Among the latter some are *impossible* and others are possible. And a possible world is a possible state of affairs. Of course not every possible state of affairs is a possible world; *Hubert's having run a mile in four minutes* is a possible state of affairs but not a possible world. No doubt it is an *element* of many possible worlds, but it isn't itself inclusive enough to be one. To be a possible world, a state of affairs must be very large—so large as to be *complete* or *maximal.*

To get at this idea of completeness we need a couple of definitions. As we have already seen (above, p. 22) a state of affairs *A* *includes* a state of affairs *B* if it is not possible that *A* obtain and *B* not obtain or if the conjunctive state of affairs *A but not B*—the state of affairs that obtains if and only if *A* obtains and *B* does not—is not possible. For example, *Jim Whittaker's being the first American to climb Mt. Everest* includes *Jim Whittaker's being an American.* It also includes *Mt. Everest's being climbed, something's being climbed, no American's having climbed Everest before Whittaker did,* and the like. *Inclusion* among states of affairs is like *entailment* among propositions; and where a state of affairs *A* includes a state of affairs *B*, the proposition corresponding to *A* entails the one corresponding to *B*. Accordingly, *Jim Whittaker is the first American to climb Everest* entails *Mt. Everest has been climbed, something has been climbed,* and *no American climbed Everest before Whittaker did.* Now suppose we say further that a state of affairs *A* *precludes* a state of affairs *B* if it is not possible that *both* obtain, or if the conjunctive state of affairs *A and B* is impossible. Thus *Whittaker's being the first American to climb Mt. Everest* precludes *Luther Jerstad's being the first American to climb Everest,* as well as *Whittaker's never having climbed any mountains.* If *A* precludes *B,* then *A*'s corresponding proposition entails the denial of the one corresponding to *B.* Still further, let's say that the *complement* of a state of affairs is the state of affairs that obtains just in case *A* does not obtain. [Or we might say that the complement (call it $\overline{A}$) of *A* is the state of affairs corresponding to the *denial* or *negation* of the proposition corresponding to *A.*] Given these definitions, we can say what it is for a state of affairs to be *complete: A* is a complete state of affairs if and only if for every state of affairs *B,* either *A includes B or A precludes B.* (We could express the same thing by saying that if *A* is a complete state of affairs, then for every state of affairs *B,* either *A* includes *B* or *A* includes $\overline{B}$, the complement of *B.*) And now we are able to say what a possible world is: a possible world is any possible state of affairs that is complete. If *A* is a possible world, then it says something about everything; every state of affairs *S* is either included in or precluded by it.

Corresponding to each possible world *W,* furthermore, there is a set of propositions that I'll call *the book on W.* A proposition is in the book on *W* just in case the state of affairs to which it corresponds is included in *W.* Or we might express it like this. Suppose we say that a proposition *P* is *true in a world W* if and only if *P would have been true if W had been actual*—if and only if, that is, it is not possible that *W* be actual and *P* be false. Then the book on *W* is the set of propositions true in *W.* Like possible worlds, books are *complete;* if *B* is a book, then for any proposition *P,* either *P* or the denial of *P* will be a member of *B.* A book is a *maximal consistent set* of propositions; it is so large that the addition of another proposition to it always yields an explicitly inconsistent set.

Of course, for each possible world there is exactly one book corresponding to it (that is, for a given world *W* there is just one book *B* such that each member of *B* is true in *W*); and for each book there is just one world to which it corresponds. So every world has its book.

It should be obvious that exactly one possible world is actual. At _least_ one must be, since the set of true propositions is a maximal consistent set and hence a book. But then it corresponds to a possible world, and the possible world corresponding to this set of propositions (since it's the set of _true_ propositions) will be actual. On the other hand there is at _most_ one actual world. For suppose there were two: W and W'. These worlds cannot include all the very same states of affairs; if they did, they would be the very same world. So there must be at least one state of affairs S such that W includes S and W' does not. But a possible world is maximal; W', therefore, includes the complement $\bar{S}$ of S. So if both W and W' were actual, as we have supposed, then both S and $\bar{S}$ would be actual—which is impossible. So there can't be more than one possible world that is actual

Leibniz pointed out that a proposition p is necessary if it is true in every possible world. We may add that p is possible if it is true in one world and impossible if true in none. Furthermore, p _entails_ q if there is no possible world in which p is true and q is false; and p _is consistent with_ q if there is at least one world in which both p and q are true.

A further feature of possible worlds is that people (and other things) _exist_ in them. Each of us exists in the actual world, obviously; but a person also exists in many worlds distinct from the actual world. It would be a mistake, of course, to think of all of these worlds as somehow "going on" at the same time, with the same person reduplicated through these worlds and actually existing in a lot of different ways. This is not what is meant by saying that the same person exists in different possible worlds. What is meant, instead, is this: a person Paul exists in each of those possible worlds W which is such that, if W _had been actual,_ Paul would have existed—actually existed. Suppose Paul had been an inch taller than he is, or a better tennis player. Then the world that does in fact obtain would not have been actual; some other world—W', let's say —would have obtained instead. If W' had been actual, Paul would have existed; so Paul exists in W'. (Of course there are still other possible worlds in which Paul does not exist—worlds, for example, in which there are no people at all.) Accordingly, when we say that Paul exists in a world

W, what we mean is that Paul *would have* existed had *W* been actual. Or we could put it like this: Paul exists in each world *W* that includes the state of affairs consisting in Paul's existence. We can put this still more simply by saying that Paul exists in those worlds whose books contain the proposition *Paul exists.*

But isn't there a problem here? *Many* people are named "Paul": Paul the apostle, Paul J. Zwier, John Paul Jones, and many other famous Pauls. So who goes with "Paul exists"? Which Paul? The answer has to do with the fact that books contain *propositions*—not sentences. They contain the sort of thing sentences are used to express and assert. And the same sentence—"Aristotle is wise," for example—can be used to express many different propositions. When Plato used it, he asserted a proposition predicating wisdom of his famous pupil; when Jackie Onassis uses it, she asserts a proposition predicating wisdom of her wealthy husband. These are distinct propositions (we might even think they differ in truth value); but they are expressed by the same sentence. Normally (but not always) we don't have much trouble determining which of the several propositions expressed by a given sentence is relevant in the context at hand. So in this case a given person, Paul, exists in a world *W* if and only if *W*'s book contains the proposition that says that *he*—that particular person—exists. The fact that the sentence we use to express this proposition can also be used to express *other* propositions is not relevant.

After this excursion into the nature of books and worlds we can return to our question. Could God have created just any world He chose? Before addressing the question, however, we must note that God does not, strictly speaking, *create* any possible worlds or states of affairs at all. What He creates are the heavens and the earth and all that they contain. But He has not created states of affairs. There are, for example, the state of affairs consisting in God's existence and the state of affairs consisting in His nonexistence. That is, there is such a thing as the state of affairs consisting in the existence of God, and there is also such a thing as the state of affairs consisting in the nonexistence of God, just as there are the two propositions *God exists* and *God does not exist.* The theist believes that the first state of affairs is actual and the first proposition true; the atheist believes that the second state of affairs is actual and the second proposition true. But, of course, both propositions *exist*, even though just one is true. Similarly, there are two states of affairs here, just one of which is actual. So both states of affairs *exist*, but only one *obtains*. And God has not created either one of them since there never was a time at which either did not exist. Nor has He created the state of affairs consisting in the earth's existence; there was a time when *the earth* did not exist, but none when the state of affairs consisting in the earth's existence didn't exist. Indeed, God did not bring into existence any states of affairs at all. What He did was to perform actions of a certain sort—creating the heavens and the earth, for example—which resulted in the *actuality* of certain states of affairs. God *actualizes* states of affairs. He actualizes the possible world that does in fact obtain; He does not create it. And while He has created Socrates, He did not create the state of affairs consisting in Socrates' existence.[16]

Bearing this in mind, let's finally return to our question. Is the atheologian right in holding that if God is omnipotent, then he could have actualized or created any possible world He pleased? Not obviously. First, we must ask ourselves whether God is a *necessary* or a *contingent* being. A *necessary* being is one that exists in every possible world—one that would have existed no matter which possible world had been actual; a contingent being exists only in some possible worlds. Now if God is not a necessary being (and many, perhaps most, theists think that He is not), then clearly enough there will be many possible worlds He could not have actualized—all those, for example, in which He does not exist. Clearly, God could not have created a world in which He doesn't even exist.

So, if God is a contingent being then there are many possible worlds

16. Strict accuracy demands, therefore, that we speak of God as *actualizing* rather than creating possible worlds. I shall continue to use both locutions, thus sacrificing accuracy to familiarity. For more about possible worlds see my book *The Nature of Necessity* (Oxford: The Clarendon Press, 1974), chaps. 4–8.

beyond His power to create. But this is really irrelevant to our present concerns. For perhaps the atheologian can maintain his case if he revises his claim to avoid this difficulty; perhaps he will say something like this: if God is omnipotent, then He could have actualized any of those possible worlds *in which He exists*. So if He exists and is omnipotent, He could have actualized (contrary to the Free Will Defense) any of those possible worlds in which He exists and in which there exist free creatures who do no wrong. He could have actualized worlds containing moral good but no moral evil. Is this correct?

Let's begin with a trivial example. You and Paul have just returned from an Australian hunting expedition: your quarry was the elusive double-wattled cassowary. Paul captured an aardvark, mistaking it for a cassowary. The creature's disarming ways have won it a place in Paul's heart; he is deeply attached to it. Upon your return to the States you offer Paul $500 for his aardvark, only to be rudely turned down. Later you ask yourself, "What would he have done if I'd offered him $700?" Now what is it, exactly, that you are asking? What you're really asking in a way is whether, under a *specific set of conditions*, Paul would have sold it. These conditions include your having offered him $700 rather than $500 for the aardvark, everything else being as much as possible like the conditions that did in fact obtain. Let S' be this set of conditions or state of affairs. S' includes the state of affairs consisting in your offering Paul $700 (instead of the $500 you did offer him); of course it does not include his *accepting* your offer, and it does not include his *rejecting* it; for the rest, the conditions it includes are just like the ones that did obtain in the actual world. So, for example, S' includes Paul's being free to accept the offer and free to refrain; and if in fact the going rate for an aardvark was $650, then S' includes the state of affairs consisting in the going rate's being $650. So we might put your question by asking which of the following conditionals is true:

(23) **If the state of affairs S' had obtained, Paul would have accepted the offer**

(24) If the state of affairs S' had obtained, Paul would not have accepted the offer.

It seems clear that at least one of these conditionals is true, but naturally they can't both be; so exactly one is.

Now since S' includes neither Paul's accepting the offer nor his rejecting it, the antecedent of (23) and (24) does not entail the consequent of either. That is,

(25) S' obtains

does not entail either

(26) Paul accepts the offer

or

(27) Paul does not accept the offer.

So there are possible worlds in which both (25) and (26) are true, and other possible worlds in which both (25) and (27) are true.

We are now in a position to grasp an important fact. Either (23) or (24) is in fact true; and either way there are possible worlds God could not have actualized. Suppose, first of all, that (23) is true. Then it was beyond the power of God to create a world in which (1) Paul is free to sell his aardvark and free to refrain, and in which the other states of affairs included in S' obtain, and (2) Paul does not sell. That is, it was beyond His power to create a world in which (25) and (27) are both true. There is at least one possible world like this, but God, despite His omnipotence, could not have brought about its actuality. For let W be such a world. To actualize W, God must bring it about that Paul is free with respect to this action, and that the other states of affairs included in S' obtain. But (23), as we are supposing, is true; so if God had actualized S' and left Paul *free* with respect to this action, he would have sold: in which case W would not have been actual. If, on the other hand, God had *brought it about* that Paul didn't sell or had *caused him* to refrain from selling, then Paul would not have been free with respect to this action; then S' would not have been actual (since S' includes

Paul's being free with respect to it), and W would not have been actual since W includes S'.

Of course if it is (24) rather than (23) that is true, then another class of worlds was beyond God's power to actualize—those, namely, in which S' obtains and Paul *sells* his aardvark. These are the worlds in which both (25) and (26) are true. But either (23) or (24) is true. Therefore, there are possible worlds God could not have actualized. If we consider whether or not God could have created a world in which, let's say, both (25) and (26) are true, we see that the answer depends upon a peculiar kind of fact; it depends upon what Paul would have freely chosen to do in a certain situation. So there are any number of possible worlds such that it is partly up to Paul whether God can create them.[17]

That was a past tense example. Perhaps it would be useful to consider a future tense case, since this might seem to correspond more closely to God's situation in choosing a possible world to actualize. At some time t in the near future Maurice will be free with respect to some insignificant action—having freeze-dried oatmeal for breakfast, let's say. That is, at time t Maurice will be free to have oatmeal but also free to take something else—shredded wheat, perhaps. Next, suppose we consider S', a state of affairs that is included in the actual world and includes Maurice's being free with respect to taking oatmeal at time t. That is, S' includes Maurice's being free at time t to take oatmeal and free to reject it. S' does not include Maurice's taking oatmeal, however; nor does it include his rejecting it. For the rest S' is as much as possible like the actual world. In particular there are many conditions that do in fact hold at time t and are *relevant* to his choice—such conditions, for example, as the fact that he hasn't had oatmeal lately, that his wife will be annoyed if he rejects it, and the like; and S' includes each of these conditions. Now God no doubt knows what Maurice will do at time t, if S obtains; He knows which action Maurice would freely perform

17. For a fuller statement of this argument see Plantinga, *The Nature of Necessity*, chap. 9, secs. 4–6.

if *S* were to be actual. That is, God knows that one of the following conditionals is true:

(28) If *S'* were to obtain, Maurice will freely take the oatmeal

or

(29) If *S'* were to obtain, Maurice will freely reject it.

We may not know which of these is true, and Maurice himself may not know; but presumably God does.

So either God knows that (28) is true, or else He knows that (29) is. Let's suppose it is (28). Then there is a possible world that God, though omnipotent, cannot create. For consider a possible world *W'* that shares *S'* with the actual world (which for ease of reference I'll name "Kronos") and in which Maurice does *not* take oatmeal. (We know there *is* such a world, since *S'* does not include Maurice's taking the oatmeal.) *S'* obtains in *W'* just as it does in Kronos. Indeed, everything in *W'* is just as it is in Kronos up to time *t*. But whereas in Kronos Maurice takes oatmeal at time *t*, in *W'* he does not. Now *W'* is a perfectly possible world; but it is not within God's power to create it or bring about its actuality. For to do so He must actualize *S'*. But (28) is in fact true. So if God actualizes *S'* (as He must to create *W'*) and leaves Maurice free with respect to the action in question, then he will take the oatmeal; and then, of course, *W'* will not be actual. If, on the other hand, God causes Maurice to *refrain* from taking the oatmeal, then he is not *free* to take it. That means, once again, that *W'* is not actual; for in *W'* Maurice is free to take the oatmeal (even if he doesn't do so). So if (28) is true, then this world *W'* is one that God can't actualize; it is not within His power to actualize it even though He is omnipotent and it is a possible world.

Of course, if it is (29) that is true, we get a similar result; then too there are possible worlds that God can't actualize. These would be worlds which share *S'* with Kronos and in which Maurice *does* take oatmeal. But either (28) or (29) *is* true; so either way there is a possible world that God can't create. If we consider a world in which S' obtains and in which Maurice freely chooses oatmeal at time t, we see that whether or not it is within God's power to actualize it depends upon what Maurice would do if he were free in a certain situation. Accordingly, there are any number of possible worlds such that it is partly up to Maurice whether or not God can actualize them. It is, of course, up to God whether or not to create Maurice and also up to God whether or not to make him free with respect to the action of taking oatmeal at time t. (God could, if He chose, cause him to succumb to the dreaded *equine obsession*, a condition shared by some people and most horses, whose victims find it *psychologically impossible* to refuse oats or oat products.) But if He creates Maurice and creates him free with respect to this action, then whether or not he actually performs the action is up to Maurice—not God.[18]

Now we can return to the Free Will Defense and the problem of evil. The Free Will Defender, you recall, insists on the possibility that it is not within God's power to create a world containing moral good without creating one containing moral evil. His atheological opponent—Mackie, for example—agrees with Leibniz in insisting that *if* (as the theist holds) God is omnipotent, then it *follows* that He could have created any possible world He pleased. We now see that this contention—call it "Leibniz' Lapse"—is a mistake. The atheologian is right in holding that there are many possible worlds containing moral good but no moral evil; his mistake lies in endorsing Leibniz' Lapse. So one of his premises—that God, if omnipotent, could have actualized just any world He pleased—is false.

18. For a more complete and more exact statement of this argument see Plantinga, *The Nature of Necessity*, chap. 9, secs. 4–6.

6. Could God Have Created a World Containing Moral Good but No Moral Evil?

Now suppose we recapitulate the logic of the situation. The Free Will Defender claims that the following is possible:

(30) God is omnipotent, and it was not within His power to create a world containing moral good but no moral evil.

By way of retort the atheologian insists that there are possible worlds containing moral good but no moral evil. He adds that an omnipotent being could have actualized any possible world he chose. So if God is omnipotent, it follows that He could have actualized a world containing moral good but no moral evil; hence (30), contrary to the Free Will Defender's claim, is not possible. What we have seen so far is that his second premiss—Leibniz' Lapse—is false.

Of course, this does not settle the issue in the Free Will Defender's favor. Leibniz' Lapse (appropriately enough for a lapse) is false; but this doesn't show that (30) is possible. To show this latter we must demonstrate the possibility that among the worlds God could not have actualized are all the worlds containing moral good but no moral evil. How can we approach this question?

Instead of choosing oatmeal for breakfast or selling an aardvark, suppose we think about a morally significant action such as taking a bribe. Curley Smith, the mayor of Boston, is opposed to the proposed freeway route; it would require destruction of the Old North Church along with some other antiquated and structurally unsound buildings. L. B. Smedes, the director of highways, asks him whether he'd drop his opposition for $1 million. "Of course," he replies. "Would you do it for $2?" asks Smedes. "What do you take me for?" comes the indignant reply. "That's already established," smirks Smedes; "all that remains is to nail down your price." Smedes then offers him a bribe of $35,000; unwilling to break with the fine old traditions of Bay State politics, Curley accepts. Smedes then spends a sleepless night wondering whether he could have bought Curley for $20,000.

Now suppose we assume that Curley was free with respect to the action of taking the bribe—free to take it and free to refuse. And suppose, furthermore, that he would have taken it. That is, let us suppose that

(31) If Smedes had offered Curley a bribe of $20,000, he would have accepted it.

If (31) is true, then there is a state of affairs S' that (1) includes Curley's being offered a bribe of $20,000; (2) does not include either his accepting the bribe or his rejecting it; and (3) is otherwise as much as possible like the actual world. Just to make sure S' includes every relevant circumstance, let us suppose that it is a *maximal world segment.* That is, add to S' any state of affairs compatible with but not included in it, and the result will be an entire possible world. We could think of it roughly like this: S' is included in at least one world W in which Curley takes the bribe and in at least one world W' in which he rejects it. If S' is a maximal world segment, then S' is what remains of W when *Curley's taking the bribe* is deleted; it is also what remains of W' when *Curley's rejecting the bribe* is deleted. More exactly, if S' is a maximal world segment, then every possible state of affairs that includes S', but isn't included by S', is a possible world. So if (31) is true, then there is a maximal world segment S' that (1) includes Curley's being offered a bribe of $20,000; (2) does not include either his accepting the bribe or his rejecting it; (3) is otherwise as much as possible like the actual world —in particular, it includes Curley's being free with respect to the bribe; and (4) is such that if it were actual then Curley would have taken the bribe. That is,

(32) If S' were actual, Curley would have accepted the bribe

is true.

Now, of course, there is at least one possible world W' in which S' is actual and Curley does not take the bribe. But God could not have created W'; to do so, He would have been obliged to actualize S', leaving Curley free with respect to the action of taking the bribe. But under these conditions Curley, as (32) assures us, would have accepted the bribe, so that the world thus created would not have been S'.

Curley, as we see, is not above a bit of Watergating. But there may be worse to come. Of course, there are possible worlds in which he is significantly free (i.e., free with respect to a morally significant action) and never does what is wrong. But the sad truth about Curley may be this. Consider W', any of these worlds: in W' Curley is significantly free, so in W' there are some actions that are morally significant for him and with respect to which he is free. But at least one of these actions —call it A—has the following peculiar property. There is a maximal world segment S' that obtains in W' and is such that (1) S' includes Curley's being free re A but neither his performing A nor his refraining from A; (2) S' is otherwise as much as possible like W'; and (3) if S' had been actual, Curley would have gone wrong with respect to A.[19] (Notice that this third condition holds in fact, in the actual world; it does not hold in that world W''.)

This means, of course, that God could not have actualized W'. For to do so He'd have been obliged to bring it about that S' is actual; but then Curley would go wrong with respect to A. Since in W' he always does what is right, the world thus actualized would not be W'. On the other hand, if God causes Curley to go right with respect to A or brings it about that he does so, then Curley isn't free with respect to A; and so once more it isn't W' that is actual. Accordingly God cannot create W'. But W' was just any of the worlds in which Curley is significantly free but always does only what is right. It therefore follows that it was not within God's power to create a world in which Curley produces moral good but no moral evil. Every world God can actualize is such that if Curley is significantly free in it, he takes at least one wrong action.

19. A person goes wrong with respect to an action if he either wrongfully performs it or wrongfully fails to perform it.

Obviously Curley is in serious trouble. I shall call the malady from which he suffers *transworld depravity*. (I leave as homework the problem of comparing transworld depravity with what Calvinists call "total depravity.") By way of explicit definition:

(33) A person *P* *suffers from transworld depravity* if and only if the following holds: for every world *W* such that *P* is significantly free in *W* and *P* does only what is right in *W*, there is an action *A* and a maximal world segment *S'* such that

(1) *S'* includes *A*'s being morally significant for *P*
(2) *S'* includes *P*'s being free with respect to *A*
(3) *S'* is included in *W* and includes neither *P*'s performing *A* nor *P*'s refraining from performing *A*

and

(4) If *S'* were actual, *P* would go wrong with respect to *A*.

(In thinking about this definition, remember that (4) is to be true in fact, in the actual world—not in that world *W*.)

What is important about the idea of transworld depravity is that if a person suffers from it, then it wasn't within God's power to actualize any world in which that person is significantly free but does no wrong —that is, a world in which he produces moral good but no moral evil.

We have been considering a crucial contention of the Free Will Defender: the contention, namely, that

(30) God is omnipotent, and it was not within His power to create a world containing moral good but no moral evil.

How is transworld depravity relevant to this? As follows. Obviously it is possible that there be persons who suffer from transworld depravity. More generally, it is possible that *everybody* suffers from it. And if this possibility were actual, then God, though omnipotent, could not have created any of the possible worlds containing just the persons who do in fact exist, and containing moral good but no moral evil. For to do so He'd have to create persons who were significantly free (otherwise there would be no moral good) but suffered from transworld depravity. Such persons go wrong with respect to at least one action in any world God could have actualized and in which they are free with respect to morally significant actions; so the price for creating a world in which they produce moral good is creating one in which they also produce moral evil.

7. Transworld Depravity and Essence

Now we might think this settles the question in favor of the Free Will Defender. But the fact is it doesn't. For suppose all the people that exist in Kronos, the actual world, suffer from transworld depravity; it doesn't follow that God could not have created a world containing moral good without creating one containing moral evil. God could have created *other people*. Instead of creating us, i.e., the people that exist in Kronos, He could have created a world containing people, but not containing any of us—or perhaps a world containing some of us along with some others who do not exist in Kronos. And perhaps if He'd done that, He could have created a world containing moral good but no moral evil.

Perhaps. But then again, perhaps not. Suppose we look into the matter a little further. Let W be a world distinct from Kronos that contains a significantly free person x who does not exist in Kronos. Let us suppose that this person x does only what is right. I can see no reason to doubt that there *are* such worlds; but what reason do we have for supposing that God could have created any of them? How do we know that He can? To investigate this question, we must look into the idea of an *individual nature* or *essence*. I said earlier (p. 37) that the same individual—Socrates, for example—exists in many different possible worlds. In some of these he has properties quite different from those he has in Kronos, the actual world. But some of his properties are ones he has in every world in which he exists; these are his *essential* properties.[20] Among them would be some that are *trivially* essential—such properties

20. For a discussion of essential properties see Plantinga, *The Nature of Necessity*, chaps. 2–4.

as *being unmarried if a bachelor, being either six feet tall or else not six feet tall, being self-identical,* and the like. Another and more interesting kind of essential property can be explained as follows. Socrates has the property of being snubnosed. This property, presumably, is not essential to him; he could have had some other kind of nose. So there are possible worlds in which he is not snubnosed. Let *W'* be any such world. If *W'* had been actual, Socrates would not have been snubnosed; that is to say, Socrates has the property *being nonsnubnosed in W'*. For to say that an object *x* has a property of this sort—the property of having *P* in *W*, where *P* is a property and *W* is a possible world—is to say simply that *x would have had P if W had been actual.* Properties of this sort are *world-indexed* properties.[21] Socrates has the world-indexed property *being nonsnubnosed in W'*. He has this property in Kronos, the actual world. On the other hand, in *W'* Socrates has the property *being snubnosed in Kronos*. For suppose *W'* had been actual: then, while Socrates would not have been snubnosed, it would have been true that if *Kronos* had been actual, Socrates would have been snubnosed.

It is evident, I take it, that if indeed Socrates *is* snubnosed in Kronos, the actual world, then it is true in every world that Socrates is *snubnosed in Kronos*.[22] So he has the property *being snubnosed in Kronos* in every world in which he exists. This property, therefore, is essential to him; there is no world in which he exists and lacks it. Indeed, it is easy to see, I think, that every world-indexed property he has will be essential to him; and every world-indexed property he *lacks* will be such that its complement is essential to him.

But how many world-indexed properties does he have? Quite a few. We should note that for any world *W* and property *P*, there is the world-indexed property *has P in W*; and for any such world-indexed property, either Socrates has it or he has its complement—the property

21. For more about world-indexed properties see Plantinga, *The Nature of Necessity*, chap. 4, sec. 11.

22. For argument see Alvin Plantinga, "World and Essence," *Philosophical Review* 79 (October 1970): 487 and *The Nature of Necessity*, chap. 4, sec. 11.

of *not* having P in W. For any world W and property P, either Socrates would have had P, had W been actual, or it's false that Socrates would have had P under that condition. So each world-indexed property P is such that either Socrates has P essentially, or else its complement $\bar{P}$ is essential to him.

Now suppose we define Socrates' *essence* as the set of properties essential to him. His essence is a set of properties, each of which is essential to him; and this set contains all his world-indexed properties, together with some others. But furthermore, it is evident, I think, that no *other* person has all of these properties in this set. Another person might have *some* of the same world-indexed properties as Socrates; he might be *snubnosed in Kronos* for example. But he couldn't have *all* of Socrates' world-indexed properties for then he would just *be Socrates.* So there is no person who shares Socrates' essence with him. But we can say something even stronger: there *couldn't* be any such person. For such a person would just be Socrates and hence not *another* person. The essence of Socrates, therefore, is a set of properties each of which he has essentially. Furthermore, there neither is nor could be another person distinct from Socrates that has all of the properties in this set. And finally, Socrates' essence contains a *complete* set of world-indexed properties—that is, if P is world-indexed, then either P is a member of Socrates' essence or else $\bar{P}$ is.[23]

Returning to Curley, we recall that he suffers from transworld depravity. This fact implies something interesting about Curleyhood, Curley's essence. Take those worlds W such that *is significantly free in W and never does what is wrong in W* are contained in Curley's essence. Each of these worlds has an important property if Curley suffers from transworld depravity; each is such that God could not have created or actualized it. We can see this as follows. Suppose W' is some world such that Curley's essence contains the property *is significantly free in W' but never does what is wrong in W'.* That is, W' is a world in which Curley is significantly free but always does what is right. But, of course, Curley

---

23. For more discussion of essences see Plantinga, *The Nature of Necessity*, chap. 5.

suffers from transworld depravity. This means that there is an action
A and a maximal world segment *S'* such that

(1) *S'* includes *A*'s being morally significant for Curley
(2) *S'* includes Curley's being free with respect to *A*
(3) *S'* is included in *W'* but includes neither Curley's performing *A* nor
his refraining from *A*

and

(4) If *S'* had been actual, Curley would have gone wrong with respect
to *A*.

But then (by the argument of p. 47) God could not have created or
instantiated *W'*. For to do so he would have had to bring it about that
S' obtain; and then Curley would have gone wrong with respect to
A. Since in *W'* he always does what is right, *W'* would not have been
actual. So if Curley suffers from transworld depravity, then Curley's
essence has this property: God could not have created any world *W* such
that Curleyhood contains the properties *is significantly free in W* and
always does what is right in W.

We can use this connection between Curley's transworld depravity
and his essence as the basis for a definition of transworld depravity as
applied to essences rather than persons. We should note first that if *E*
is a person's essence, then that person is the *instantiation* of *E*; he is
the thing that has (or exemplifies) every property in *E*. To instantiate
an essence, God creates a person who has that essence; and in creating
a person He instantiates an essence. Now we can say that

(34) An essence *E suffers from transworld depravity* if and only if for
every world *W* such that *E* contains the properties *is significantly free
in W* and *always does what is right in W*, there is an action *A* and a
maximal world segment *S'* such that

(1) *S'* includes *E's being instantiated* and *E's instantiation's being free
with respect to A* and *A's being morally significant for E's instantiation,*

(2) S' is included in W but includes neither E's *instantiation's performing* A nor E's *instantiation's refraining from* A

and

(3) if S' were actual, then the instantiation of E would have gone wrong with respect to A.

By now it is evident, I take it, that if an essence E suffers from transworld depravity, then it was not within God's power to actualize a possible world W such that E contains the properties *is significantly free in W* and *always does what is right in W*. Hence it was not within God's power to create a world in which E is instantiated and in which its instantiation is significantly free but always does what is right.

And the interesting fact here is this: it is possible that every creaturely essence—every essence including the property of being created by God —suffers from transworld depravity. But now suppose this is true. Now God can create a world containing moral good only by creating significantly free persons. And, since every person is the instantiation of an essence, He can create significantly free persons only by instantiating some essences. But if every essence suffers from transworld depravity, then no matter which essences God instantiates, the resulting persons, if free with respect to morally significant actions, would always perform at least some wrong actions. If every essence suffers from transworld depravity, then it was beyond the power of God Himself to create a world containing moral good but no moral evil. He might have been able to create worlds in which moral evil is very considerably outweighed by moral good; but it was not within His power to create worlds containing moral good but no moral evil—and this despite the fact that He is omnipotent. Under these conditions God could have created a world containing no moral evil only by creating one without significantly free persons. But it is possible that every essence suffers from transworld depravity; so it's possible that God could not have created a world containing moral good but no moral evil.

8. The Free Will Defense Vindicated

Put formally, you remember, the Free Will Defender's project was to show that

(1) God is omniscient, omnipotent, and wholly good

is consistent with

(3) There is evil.

What we have just seen is that

(35) It was not within God's power to create a world containing moral good but no moral evil

is possible and consistent with God's omnipotence and omniscience. But then it is clearly consistent with (1). So we can use it to show that (1) is consistent with (3). For consider

(1) God is omnipotent, omniscient, and wholly good
(35) It was not within God's power to create a world containing moral good without creating one containing moral evil

and

(36) God created a world containing moral good.

These propositions are evidently consistent—i.e., their conjunction is a possible proposition. But taken together they entail

(3) There is evil.

For (36) says that God created a world containing moral good; this together with (35) entails that He created one containing moral evil. But if it contains moral evil, then it contains evil. So (1), (35), and (36) are jointly consistent and entail (3); hence (1) is consistent with (3); hence set A is consistent. Remember: to serve in this argument (35) and (36) need not be known to be true, or likely on our evidence, or anything of the sort; they need only be consistent with (1). Since they are, there is no contradiction in set A; so the Free Will Defense appears to be successful.

9. Is God's Existence Compatible with the Amount of Moral Evil the World Contains?

The world, after all, contains a *great deal* of moral evil; and what we've seen so far is only that God's existence is compatible with *some* moral evil. Perhaps the atheologian can regroup; perhaps he can argue that at any rate God's existence is not consistent with the vast *amount* and *variety* of moral evil the universe actually contains. Of course, there doesn't seem to be any way to measure moral evil—that is, we don't have units like volts or pounds or kilowatts so that we could say "this situation contains exactly 35 turps of moral evil." Still, we can compare situations in terms of evil, and we can often see that one state of affairs contains more moral evil than another. Now perhaps the atheologian could maintain that at any rate God could have created a world containing *less* moral evil than the actual world contains.

But is this really obvious? It is obvious, but, considered by itself it is also irrelevant. God could have created a world with *no* moral evil just by creating no significantly free creatures. A more relevant question is this: was it within God's power to create a world that contained a better mixture of moral good and evil than Kronos—one, let's say, that contained as much moral good but less moral evil? And here the answer is not obvious at all. Possibly this was *not* within God's power, which is all the Free Will Defender needs. We can see this as follows. Of course, there are many possible worlds containing as much moral good as Kronos, but less moral evil. Let *W'* be any such world. If *W'* had been actual, there would have been as much moral good (past, present, and future) as in fact there was, is, and will be; and there would have been less moral evil in all. Now in *W'* a certain set S of essences is instantiated (that is, there is a set S of essences such that if *W'* had been actual, then each member of S would have been instantiated). So to create W' God would have had to create persons who were the instantiations of these essences. The following, however, is possible. There is an action A, a maximal world segment S' and a member E of S such that

> (a) E contains the properties: *is significantly free with respect to A in W'* and *goes right with respect to A in W'*
>
> (b) S' is included in W' and includes *E's being instantiated,* but includes neither *E's instantiation's performing A* nor *E's instantiation's refraining from A*

and

> (c) if S' had been actual, E's instantiation would have gone wrong with respect to A.

If this possibility is actual, then God could not have actualized W'. For to do so He'd have had to instantiate E, cause E's instantiation to be free with respect to A, and bring it about that S' was actual. But then the instantiation of E would have gone wrong with respect to A, so that the world thus created would not have been W'; for in W' E's instantiation goes *right* with respect to A.

More generally, it's possible that every world containing as much moral good as the actual world, but less moral evil, resembles W' in that God could not have created it. For it is possible that

> (37) For every world W containing as much moral good as Kronos, but less moral evil, there is at least one essence E, an action A, and a maximal world segment S' such that
>
> (1) E contains the properties: *is free with respect to A in W* and *goes right with respect to A in W*
>
> (2) S' is included in W and includes E's being instantiated but includes neither *E's instantiation's performing A* nor *E's instantiation's refraining from A*

and

> (3) if S' were actual, E's <u>instantiation</u> would have gone wrong with respect to A.

↳ providing concrete evidence in support of a theory, concept, claim...

(37) is possible; if it is *true*, then it wasn't within the power of God to create a world containing as much moral good as this one but less moral evil. So it's possible that this was not within God's power; but if so, then (1) is compatible with the proposition that there is as much moral evil as Kronos does in fact contain. And, of course, what the Free Will Defender claims is not that (37) is *true;* he claims only that it is compatible with the existence of a wholly good, omnipotent God.

The Free Will Defense, then successfully shows that set *A* is consistent. It can also be used to show that

(1) God is omnipotent, omniscient, and morally perfect

is consistent with

(38) There is as much moral evil as Kronos contains.

For clearly enough (1), (37), and

(39) God has created a world containing as much moral good as Kronos contains

are jointly consistent. But (37) tells us that God could not have created a world containing more moral good but less moral evil than Kronos; so these three propositions entail (38). It follows that (1) and (38) are consistent.

10. Is God's Existence Compatible with Natural Evil?

Perhaps the atheologian can regroup once more. What about *natural evil?* Evil that can't be ascribed to the free actions of human beings? Suffering due to earthquakes, disease, and the like? Is the existence of evil of *this sort* compatible with (1)? Here two lines of thought present themselves. On the one hand, it is conceivable that some natural evils and some persons are so related that the persons would have produced *less* moral good if the evils had been absent. Some people deal creatively with certain kinds of hardship or suffering, acting in such a way that on balance the whole state of affairs is valuable. And perhaps the response would have been less impressive and the total situation less valuable if the evil had not taken place. But a more traditional line of thought is indicated by St. Augustine (p. 26), who attributes much of the evil we find to *Satan* or to Satan and his cohorts. Satan, so the traditional doctrine goes, is a mighty nonhuman spirit who, along with many other angels, was created long before God created man. Unlike most of his colleagues, Satan rebelled against God and has since been wreaking whatever havoc he can. The result is natural evil. So the natural evil we find is due to free actions of nonhuman spirits.

Augustine is presenting what I earlier called a *theodicy*, as opposed to a *defense*. He believes that *in fact* natural evil (except for what can be attributed to God's punishment) is to be ascribed to the activity of beings that are free and rational but nonhuman. The Free Will Defender, of course, does not assert that this is *true;* he says only that it is *possible* [(and consistent with (1)]. He points to the possibility that natural evil is due to the actions of significantly free but nonhuman persons. We have noted that there is no inconsistency in the idea that God could not have created a world with a better balance of moral good over moral evil than this one displays. Something similar holds here; possibly natural evil is due to the free activity of nonhuman persons; and possibly it wasn't within God's power to create a set of such persons whose free actions produced a greater balance of good over evil. That is to say, it is possible that

> (40) Natural evil is due to the free actions of nonhuman persons; there is a balance of good over evil with respect to the actions of these nonhuman persons; and it was not within the power of God to create a world that contains a more favorable balance of good over evil with respect to the actions of the nonhuman persons it contains.

Again, it must be emphasized that (40) is not required to be *true* for the success of the Free Will Defense; it need only be compatible with (1). And it certainly looks as if it is. If (40) *is* true, furthermore, then *natural* evil significantly resembles *moral* evil in that, like the latter, it is the result of the activity of significantly free persons. In fact both moral and natural evil would then be special cases of what we might call *broadly moral evil*—evil resulting from the free actions of personal beings, whether human or not. Given this idea, we can combine (37) and (40) into one compendious statement:

(41) **All the evil in Kronos is broadly moral evil, and it was not within the power of God to create a world containing a better balance of broadly moral good and evil.**

(41) appears to be consistent with (1) and

(42) **God creates a world containing as much broadly moral good as Kronos contains.**

But (1), (41), and (42) together entail that there is as much evil as Kronos contains. So (1) is consistent with the proposition that there is as much evil as Kronos contains. I therefore conclude that the Free Will Defense successfully rebuts the charge of inconsistency brought against the theist.

11. Does the Existence of Evil Make It Unlikely That God Exists?

Not all atheologians who argue that one can't rationally accept the existence of both God and evil, maintain that there is *inconsistency* here. Another possibility is that the existence of evil, or of the amount of it we find (perhaps coupled with other things we know) makes it *unlikely* or *improbable* that God exists. And, of course, this could be true even if the existence of God is consistent with that of evil. In *Philosophical Problems and Arguments* James Cornman and Keith Lehrer concede that the amount of evil we find in the actual world is consistent with the existence of God; they argue, however, that the latter is unlikely or improbable, given the former. The essence of their contention is found in the following passage:

If you were all-good, all-knowing, and all-powerful, and you were going to create a universe in which there were sentient beings—beings that are happy and sad; enjoy pleasure; feel pain; express love, anger, pity, hatred —what kind of world would you create? Being all-powerful, you would have the ability to create any world that it is logically possible for you to create, and being all-knowing you would know how to create any of these logically possible worlds. Which one would you choose? Obviously you would choose the best of all the possible worlds because you would be all-good and would want to do what is best in everything you do. You would, then, create the best of all the possible worlds, that is, that world containing the least amount of evil possible. And because one of the most obvious kinds of evil is suffering, hardship, and pain, you would create a world in which the sentient things suffered the least. Try to imagine what such a world would be like. Would it be like the one which actually does exist, this world we live in? Would you create a world such as this one if you had the power and knowhow to create any logically possible world? If your answer is "no," as it seems it must be, then you should begin to understand why the evil of suffering and pain in this world is such a problem for anyone who thinks God created this world; then, it seems we should conclude that it is improbable that it was created or sustained by anything we would call God. Thus, given this particular world, it seems we should conclude that it is improbable that God—who if he exists, created the world—exists. Consequently, the belief that God does not exist, rather than the belief that he exists, would seem to be justified by the evidence we find in this world.[24]

"Would you create a world such as this one," ask Cornman and Lehrer, "if you had the power and knowhow to create any logically possible world?" One premise of their argument, then, seems to be

(43) If God is omnipotent and omniscient, then He could have created any logically possible world.

But further, ". . . you would choose the best of all the possible worlds because you would be all-good and would want to do what is best in everything you do." So another premise of their argument is

(44) If God is all-good, He would choose to create the best world He could.

24. James Cornman and Keith Lehrer, *Philosophical Problems and Arguments* (New York: Macmillan Co., 1969), pp. 340–349.

From (43) and (44) they apparently conclude

(45) If God is omniscient, omnipotent, and all-good, He would have created the best of all possible worlds.

But, they add,

(46) It is unlikely or improbable that the actual world is the best of all possible worlds.

And from (45) and (46) it follows that it is unlikely or improbable that there is an omnipotent, omniscient, and all-good God.

The first premise of this argument is another statement of Leibniz' Lapse; and we have already seen that the latter is false. It isn't true that God, if omnipotent, could have actualized just any possible world. The inference of (15) from (13) and (11), furthermore, seems to presuppose that there *is* such a thing as the best of all possible worlds; and we have already seen that this supposition is suspect. Just as there is no greatest prime number, so perhaps there is no best of all possible worlds. Perhaps for any world you mention, replete with dancing girls and deliriously happy sentient creatures, there is an even better world, containing even more dancing girls and deliriously happy sentient creatures. If so, it seems reasonable to think that the second possible world is better than the first. But then it follows that for any possible world W there is a better world W', in which case there just isn't any such thing as the best of all possible worlds.

So this argument is not at all satisfactory. How, indeed, *could* one argue, from the existence of evil, that it is unlikely that God exists? I certainly don't see how to do it. As a matter of fact I think I see how to argue that the amount and variety of the evil we find does *not* make the existence of God improbable. Take another look at

(41) All the evil in Kronos is broadly moral evil; and of all the worlds God could have created, none contains a better balance of broadly moral good with respect to broadly moral evil.

Now I don't know of any evidence against (41). Of course, it involves the idea that the evil which isn't due to free *human* agency, is due to the free agency of *other* rational and significantly free creatures. Many people find this idea preposterous; but that is scarcely evidence against it. Some theologians tell us that this idea is repugnant to "man come of age" or to "modern habits of thought." Again, this may be so (although it certainly isn't repugnant to *everyone* nowadays), but it doesn't come to much as evidence. The mere fact that a belief is unpopular at present (or at some other time) is interesting from a sociological point of view but evidentially irrelevant. "We have every reason to think", say Cornman and Lehrer, "that all natural evils have perfectly natural causes. It is therefore unreasonable to postulate some nonnatural cause to explain their occurrences." But, of course, here we're not *postulating* the existence of nonhuman free agents to *explain* natural evil; we're simply asking if we have evidence against (41). Perhaps, given our evidence, it would be irrational to postulate the existence of such beings; it does not follow that we have evidence *against* their existence. According to Cornman and Lehrer, we have every reason to suppose that natural evil has perfectly natural causes—where, no doubt, Satan and his minions would definitely not count as natural causes. But this is relevant only if their having natural causes precludes their *also* having nonnatural causes. What Cornman and Lehrer must mean, then, is that we have every reason to believe that these evils are *not* to be ascribed to the free activity of nonhuman rational beings. I don't know of any such reason and doubt very much that Cornman and Lehrer do either. At any rate they haven't suggested any. Perhaps they mean only that we have no reason to think that evil *is* caused by such beings. Perhaps so; but again this gives us no evidence for the proposition that it isn't so caused.

I therefore do not believe that we have evidence against (41). In particular, the existence of evil—of the amount and variety of evil we actually find—is not evidence against it. We can make this more exact as follows. Suppose we say that a proposition *p* *confirms* a proposition *q* if *q* is more probable than not on *p* alone: if, that is, *q* would be more probable than not-*q* with respect to what we know, if *p* were the only thing we knew that was relevant to *q*. And let's say that *p* *disconfirms*

q if p confirms the denial of q. And, just to facilitate discussion, let's agree that there are 10^{18} turps of evil; the total amount of evil (past, present, and future) contained by Kronos amounts to 10^{18} turps. I think it is evident that

(47) There are 10^{18} turps of evil

does not disconfirm (41). Nor does (47) disconfirm

(48) God is omniscient, omnipotent, and morally perfect; God has created the world; all the evil in the world is broadly moral evil; and there is no possible world God could have created that contains a better balance of broadly moral good with respect to broadly moral evil.

Now if a proposition p confirms a proposition q, then it confirms every proposition q entails. But then it follows that if p disconfirms q, p disconfirms every proposition that entails q. (47) does not disconfirm (48); (48) entails (1); so the existence of the amount and variety of evil actually displayed in the world does not render improbable the existence of an omniscient, omnipotent, and wholly good God. So far as this argument goes, there may be *other* things we know such that the existence of God is improbable with respect to *them*. Although I can't think of any such things, this argument doesn't show that there aren't any. But it does show that the existence of evil—specifically the amount Kronos contains—does not disconfirm God's existence.

The upshot, I believe, is that there is no good atheological argument from evil. The existence of God is neither precluded nor rendered improbable by the existence of evil. Of course, suffering and misfortune may nonetheless constitute a *problem* for the theist; but the problem is not that his beliefs are logically or probabilistically incompatible. The theist may find a *religious* problem in evil; in the presence of his own suffering or that of someone near to him he may find it difficult to maintain what he takes to be the proper attitude towards God. Faced with great personal suffering or misfortune, he may be tempted to rebel against God, to shake his fist in God's face, or even to give up belief in God altogether. But this is a problem of a different dimension. Such a problem calls, not for philosophical enlightenment, but for pastoral care. The Free Will Defense, however, shows that the existence of God is compatible, both logically and probabilistically, with the existence of evil; thus it solves the main philosophical problem of evil.

b Other Atheological Arguments

There are many other considerations people sometimes bring against theistic belief. Among these, for example, are the Freudian claim that theistic belief is a matter of wish-fulfillment and the Marxist suggestion that religion is a means whereby one segment of society oppresses another. But are the alleged facts supposed to be reasons for thinking theism is false? If so, they don't come to much. Is it a fact that those who believe in a Heavenly Father do so because or partly because their earthly fathers were inadequate? I doubt it. If it is a fact, however, it is of psychological rather than theological interest. It may help us understand theists, but it tells us nothing at all about the truth of their belief; to that it is simply irrelevant.

Verificationism is another atheological approach—one more common some years ago, perhaps, than at present. This is the claim that a sentence makes sense or is literally significant only if it can be *empirically verified*—that is, roughly, only if its truth value can be determined by the methods of natural science. Since statements about God don't meet this condition (so the claim goes), they are, strictly speaking, sheer nonsense. Since they have no content and say nothing at all, they don't even have the good fortune to be *false*. A theological sentence, in the view in question, is blatant nonsense masquerading as sensible statement.[25] In its palmy days—the 30s and 40s—verificationism enjoyed widespread

25. A classic and readable statement of verificationism is A. J. Ayer's *Language, Truth and Logic* (London: Gollancz, 1946).

acceptance as well as a delicious air of being avant-garde and with it. But nowadays few if any philosophers are willing to call themselves verificationists, perhaps for two reasons. First, it seems impossible to state the so-called "verifiability criterion" in a way which rules out theological and metaphysical statements without paying the same compliment to scientific and common sense statements. Furthermore, there seems to be no reason at all why a theist, or anyone else who holds beliefs ruled out by the verifiability criterion, should feel even the slightest obligation to accept that criterion.[26] I shall therefore say no more about this kind of atheology.

The last argument I wish to discuss is perhaps only mildly atheological. This is the claim that God's omniscience is incompatible with human freedom. Many people are inclined to think that if God is omniscient, then human beings are never free. Why? Because the idea that God is omniscient implies that at any given time God knows not only what *has* taken place and what *is* taking place, but also what *will* take place. He knows the future as well as the past. But now suppose He knows that Paul will perform some trivial action tomorrow—having an orange for lunch, let's say. If God knows in advance that Paul will have an orange for lunch tomorrow, then it must be the case that he'll have an orange tomorrow; and if it *must* be the case that Paul will have an orange tomorrow, then it isn't possible that Paul will *refrain* from so doing—in which case he won't be free to refrain, and hence won't be free with respect to the action of taking the orange. So if God knows in advance that a person will perform a certain action *A*, then that person isn't free with respect to that action. But if God is omniscient, then for any person and any action he performs, God knew in advance that he'd perform that action. So if God is omniscient, no one ever performs any free actions.

This argument may initially sound plausible, but the fact is it is based upon confusion. The central portion can be stated as follows:

26. For a critical account of verificationism see Plantinga, *God and Other Minds*, chap. 7.

(49) If God knows in advance that X will do A, then it must be the case that X will do A

and

(50) If it must be the case that X will do A, then X is not free to refrain from A.

From (49) and (50) it follows that if God knows in advance that someone will take a certain action, then that person isn't free with respect to that action. But (49) bears further inspection. Why should we think it's *true?* Because, we shall be told, if God *knows* that X will do A, it *logically follows* that X will do A: it's necessary that if God knows that p, then p is true. But this defense of (49) suggests that the latter is *ambiguous;* it may mean either

(49a) Necessarily, if God knows in advance that X will do A, then indeed X will do A

or

(49b) If God knows in advance that X will do A, then it is necessary that X will do A.

The atheological argument requires the truth of (49b); but the above defense of (49) supports only (49a), not (49b). It is indeed necessarily true that if God (or anyone else) knows that a proposition P is true, then P is true; but it simply doesn't follow that if God knows P, then P is *necessarily* true. *If I know that Henry is a bachelor, then Henry is a bachelor* is a necessary truth; it does not follow that if I know that Henry is a bachelor, then it is necessarily true that he is. I know that Henry is a bachelor. what follows is only that *Henry is married* is false; it doesn't follow that it is necessarily false.

So the claim that divine omniscience is incompatible with human freedom seems to be based upon confusion. Nelson Pike has suggested[27] an interesting revision of this old claim: he holds, not that human freedom is incompatible with God's being omniscient, but with God's

---

27. Nelson Pike, "Divine Omniscience and Voluntary Action," *Philosophical Review* 74 (January 1965): 27.

being *essentially* omniscient. Recall (p. 50) that an object X has a property P *essentially* if X has P in every world in which X exists—if, that is, it is impossible that X should have existed but *lacked P*. Now many theologians and philosophers have held that at least some of God's important properties are essential to him in this sense. It is plausible to hold, for example, that God is essentially omnipotent. Things could have gone differently in various ways; but if there had been no omnipotent being, then God would not have existed. *He* couldn't have been power-less or limited in power. But the same may be said for God's *omni-science*. If God is omniscient, then He is unlimited in knowledge; He knows every true proposition and believes none that are false. If He is *essentially* omniscient, furthermore, then He not only *is not* limited in knowledge; He *couldn't* have been. There is no possible world in which He exists but fails to know some truth or believes some falsehood. And Pike's claim is that this belief—the belief that God is essentially omnipotent—is inconsistent with human freedom.

To argue his case Pike considers the case of Jones, who mowed his lawn at T_2—last Saturday, let's say. Now suppose that God is essentially omniscient. Then at any earlier time T_1—80 years ago, for example—God believed that Jones would mow his lawn at T_2. Since He is *essentially* omniscient, furthermore, it isn't possible that God falsely believes something; hence His having believed at T_1 that Jones would mow his lawn at T_2 entails that Jones does indeed mow his lawn at T_2. Pike's argument (in his own words) then goes as follows:

1. "God existed at T_1" entails "If Jones did X at T_2, God believed at T_1 that Jones would do X at T_2."

2. "God believes X" entails "X is true."

3. It is not within one's power at a given time to do something having a description that is logically contradictory.

4. It is not within one's power at a given time to do something that would bring it about that someone who held a certain belief at a time prior to the time in question did not hold that belief at the time prior to the time in question.

PIKE'S ARGUMENT

5. It is not within one's power at a given time to do something that would bring it about that a person who existed at an earlier time did not exist at that earlier time.

6. If God existed at T_1 and if God believed at T_1 that Jones would do X at T_2, then if it was within Jones' power at T_2 to refrain from doing X, then (1) it was within Jones' power at T_2 to do something that would have brought it about that God held a false belief at T_1, or (2) it was within Jones' power at T_2 to do something which would have brought it about that God did not hold the belief He held at T_1, or (3) it was within Jones' power at T_2 to do something that would have brought it about that any person who believed at T_1 that Jones would do X at T_2 (one of whom was, by hypothesis, God) held a false belief and thus was not God—that is, that God (who by hypothesis existed at T_1) did not exist at T_1.

7. Alternative 1 in the consequent of item 6 is false (from 2 and 3).

8. Alternative 2 in the consequent of item 6 is false (from 4).

9. Alternative 3 in the consequent of item 6 is false (from 5).

10. Therefore, if God existed at T_1 and if God believed at T_1 that Jones would do X at T_2, then it was not within Jones' power at T_2 to refrain from doing X (from 1 and 10).[28]

What about this argument? The first two premises simply make explicit part of what is involved in the idea that God is essentially omniscient; so there is no quarreling with them. Premises 3–5 also seem correct. But that complicated premise (6) warrants a closer look. What exactly does it say? I think we can understand Pike here as follows. Consider

(51) God existed at T_1, and God believed at T_1 that Jones would do X at T_2, and it was within Jones' power to refrain from doing X at T_2.

What Pike means to say, I believe, is that either (51) entails

(52) It was within Jones' power at T_2 to do something that would have brought it about that God held a false belief at T_1

28. Ibid., pp. 33–34.

or (51) entails

(53) It was within Jones' power at T_2 to do something that would have brought it about that God did not hold the belief He did hold at T_1

or it entails

(54) It was within Jones' power at T_2 to do something that would have brought it about that anyone who believed at T_1 that Jones would do X at T_2 (one of whom was by hypothesis God) held a false belief and thus was not God—that is, that God (who by hypothesis existed at T_1) did not exist at T_1.

[The remainder of Pike's reasoning consists in arguing that each of (52), (53), and (54) is necessarily false, if God is essentially omniscient; hence (51) is necessarily false, if God is essentially omniscient, which means that God's being essentially omniscient is incompatible with human freedom.] Now suppose we look at these one at a time. Does (51) entail (52)? No. (52) says that it was within Jones' power to do something— namely, refrain from doing X—such that if he had done that thing, then God *would have* held a false belief at T_1. But this does not follow from (51). If Jones had refrained from X, then a proposition that God *did in fact* believe would have been false; but if Jones had refrained from X at T_2, then God (since He is omniscient) *would not have believed at* T_1 *that Jones will do X at* T_2—indeed, He would have held the true belief that Jones will *refrain* from doing X at T_2. What follows from (51) is not (52) but only (52'):

(52') It was within Jones' power to do something such that if he had done it, then a belief that God *did hold* at T_1 *would have been* false.

But (52') is not at all paradoxical and in particular does not imply that it was within Jones' power to do something that would have brought it about that God held a false belief.

Perhaps we can see this more clearly if we look at it from the vantage point of possible worlds. We are told by (51) both that in the actual world God believes that Jones does X at T_2 and also that it is within Jones' power to *refrain* from doing X at T_2. Now consider any world W in which Jones *does* refrain from doing X. In *that* world, a belief that God holds in the actual world—in Kronos—is false. That is, if W had been actual, then a belief that God does *in fact* hold would have been false. But it does not follow that in W God holds a false belief. For it doesn't follow that if W had been actual, God would have believed that Jones would do X at T_2. Indeed, if God is essentially omniscient (omniscient in every world in which He exists) what follows is that in W God did *not* believe at T_1 that Jones will do X at T_2; He believed instead that Jones will *refrain* from X. So (51) by no means implies that it was within Jones' power to bring it about that God held a false belief at T_1.

What about

(53) It was within Jones' power at T_2 to do something that would have brought it about that God did not hold the belief He did hold at T_1?

Here the first problem is one of understanding. How are we to take this proposition? One way is this. What (53) says is that it was within Jones' power, at T_2, to do something such that if he had done it, then at T_1 God would have held a certain belief and also *not* held that belief. That is, (53) so understood attributes to Jones the power to bring about a contradictory state of affairs [call this interpretation (53a)]. (53a) is obviously and resoundingly false; but there is no reason whatever to think that (51) entails it. What (51) entails is rather

(53b) It was within Jones' power at T_2 to do something such that if he had done it, then God would not have held a belief that in fact he did hold.

This follows from (51) but is perfectly innocent. For suppose again that (51) is true, and consider a world W in which Jones refrains from doing X. If God is essentially omniscient, then in this world W He is omniscient and hence does not believe at T_1 that Jones will do X at T_2. So what follows from (51) is the harmless assertion that it was within Jones' power to do something such that if he had done it, then God would not have held a belief that in fact (in the actual world) He did hold. But by no stretch of the imagination does it follow that if Jones had done it, then it would have been true that God *did* hold a belief He didn't hold. Taken one way (53) is obviously false but not a consequence of (51); taken the other it is a consequence of (51) but by no means obviously false.

(54) fares no better. What it says is that it was within Jones' power at T_2 to do something such that if he had done it, then God would not have been omniscient and thus would not have been God. But this simply doesn't follow from (51). The latter does, of course, entail

(54') It was within Jones' power to do something such that if he'd done it, then anyone who believed at T_1 that Jones would do X at T_2 would have held a false belief.

For suppose again that (51) is in fact true, and now consider one of those worlds W in which Jones refrains from doing X. In that world

(55) Anyone who believed at T_1 that Jones will do X at T_2 held a false belief

is true. That is, if W had been actual, (55) would have been true. But again in W God does not believe that Jones will do X at T_2; (55) is *true* in W but isn't relevant to God there. If Jones had refrained from X, then (55) would have been true. It does not follow that God would not have been omniscient; for in those worlds in which Jones does not do X at T_2, God does not believe at T_1 that He does.

Perhaps the following is a possible source of confusion here. If God is *essentially* omniscient, then He is omniscient in every possible world in which He exists. Accordingly there is no possible world in which He holds a false belief. Now consider any belief that God does in fact hold. It might be tempting to suppose that if He is essentially omniscient, then He holds that belief in every world in which He exists. But of course this doesn't follow. It is not essential to Him to hold the beliefs He does hold; what is essential to Him is the quite different property of holding only true beliefs. So if a belief is true in Kronos but false in some world W, then in Kronos God holds that belief and in W He does not.

Much more should be said about Pike's piece, and there remain many fascinating details. I shall leave them to you, however. And by way of concluding our study of natural atheology: none of the arguments we've examined has prospects for success; all are unacceptable. There are arguments we haven't considered, of course; but so far the indicated conclusion is that natural atheology doesn't work.

PART II
NATURAL THEOLOGY

Natural atheology, therefore, is something of a flop. We shall now turn to natural theology, a discipline of which natural atheology is a sort of inversion. Many philosophers have offered *arguments* for the existence of God; these arguments constitute an essential part of *natural theology*. Although this discipline is not now flourishing as luxuriantly as during the High Middle Ages, there are several recent books that competently carry on its tradition.[1]

According to Immanuel Kant, there are essentially three different kinds of argument for the existence of God: the cosmological argument, the teleological argument, and the ontological argument. Although this classification is not wholly adequate, it will do as a first approximation. I shall give examples of all three, commenting briefly on the first and second, and in more detail upon the third.

---

1. For just one example see James Ross' *Philosophical Theology* (New York: Bobbs-Merrill Co., Inc., 1969).

a The Cosmological Argument

Thomas Aquinas states one version of the cosmological argument as follows:

> The third way is taken from possibility and necessity and runs thus. We find in nature things that are possible to be and not to be, since they are found to be generated and to be corrupted, and consequently, it is possible for them to be and not to be. But it is impossible for these always to exist, for that which can not-be at some time is not. Therefore, if everything can not-be, then at one time there was nothing in existence. Now if this were true then even now there would be nothing in existence, because that which does not exist, begins to exist only through something already existing. Therefore if at one time nothing was in existence, it would have been impossible for anything to have begun to exist; and thus now nothing would be in existence—which is absurd. Therefore, not all beings are merely possible, but there must exist something the existence of which is necessary. But every necessary thing either has its necessity caused by another, or not. Now it is impossible to go on to infinity in necessary things which have their necessity caused by another, as has already been proved in regard to efficient causes. Therefore, we cannot but admit the existence of some being having of itself its own necessity, and not receiving it from another, but rather causing in others their necessity. This all men speak of as God.[2]

Now how could we outline this argument? What are its premises, and how does it proceed? Approximately as follows:

2. Thomas Aquinas *Summa Theologica*, q. 3, art. 3.

(1) There are at present contingent beings ("things that are possible to be and not to be").

(2) Whatever can fail to exist, at some time does not exist ("that which can not-be at some time is not"). *[handwritten: i.e. contingent beings go in & out of existence]*

(3) Therefore, if all beings are contingent, then at one time nothing existed. (2)

(4) Whatever begins to exist is caused to begin to exist by something else already existing.

(5) Therefore, if at some time *t* nothing existed, then nothing would have existed at any later time. (4) *[handwritten: (b/c something can't come from nothing)]*

(6) So if at one time nothing existed, then nothing exists now. (5)

(7) So if all beings are contingent nothing exists now. (3) and (6)

(8) Hence not all beings are contingent; there is at least one necessary being. (7) and (1)

(9) Every necessary being either has its necessity caused by another or has its necessity in itself.

(10) There cannot be an infinite series of necessary beings each having its necessity caused by another.

(11) Therefore, there is a necessary being having of itself its own necessity, and this all men speak of as God. (8), (9), and (10)

This is an interesting but puzzling argument. First of all, what is a necessary being? Well, a contingent being is one such that it's possible for it to exist and also possible for it not to exist; so presumably a necessary being is a being such that it's *not* possible for it not to exist. A necessary being exists in every possible world. Many philosophers have found the very idea of a necessary being problematic. Some even seem to find it insulting and offensive. But none has ever produced, I think, even reasonably cogent grounds for supposing that there couldn't be any such thing. And if we think of the vast variety of things the universe contains—people, properties, propositions, planets, sets, and stars—it seems plausible to think that some of them would have existed no matter which possible world had been actual. Consider, for example, the proposition *there are unicorns in the Florida Everglades*, or less specifically, *there are unicorns*. This proposition is false. If there had been unicorns, however, it would have been true. In those possible worlds in which, as in Kronos, there are no unicorns this proposition is false; in those in which there are some it is true. But in both types of world this proposition *exists*: which is only to say that there *is* such a proposition. And hence it exists in every possible world.

On the other hand, if Aquinas means to be talking about necessary beings in *this* sense—beings that exist in every possible world—it is certainly difficult to understand his distinction between beings that are necessary "in themselves" and those that have their necessity "from another." What could this mean? How could one necessary being get its necessity from another? The very idea seems to make no sense. This and other considerations suggest that perhaps after all Aquinas is not talking about a logically necessary being (one that exists in every world), but about one that has necessity of some other kind.[3] It's not very clear, however, what this kind of necessity might be. And suppose we knew, furthermore, what kind of necessity he had in mind: what leads him to think that if he's proven the existence of a being that is necessary in itself (in whatever sense of necessity he has in mind) he's proved the existence of God? In sections of the *Summa Theologica* following the passage I quoted he tries to supply some reason for thinking that a being necessary in itself would have to be God. This attempt, however, is by no means wholly successful.

An even more impressive defect in the proof comes to light when we consider (2) and its relation to (3). In the first place

(2) Whatever can fail to exist, at some time does not exist

is by no means obviously or evidently true. Why couldn't there be a contingent being that always has existed and always will exist? Is it clear that there could be no such thing? Not very. But even if we concede (2), the proof still seems to be in trouble. For

(3) If all beings are contingent, then at one time nothing existed

3. Peter Geach and G. E. M. Anscombe, *Three Philosophers* (Oxford: Oxford University Press, 1961), p. 115; and T. Patterson Brown, "St. Thomas' Doctrine of Necessary Being," *Philosophical Review* 73 (1964): 76–90 discuss this problem and suggest another kind of necessity.

doesn't follow. What (2) says is really

(2') For every contingent being B, there is a time t such that B does not exist at t

From this Aquinas appears to infer

(3') There is a time t at which no contingent beings exist.

This is a fallacious inference; it is like arguing from

For every person A there is a person B such that B is the mother of A

to

There is a person B such that for every person A, B is the mother of A.

The first seems reasonable enough, but the second is utterly outrageous; more to the present point, it does not follow from the first. Similarly here: suppose it's true that for each thing there is a time at which it does not exist; we can't properly infer that there is some one time such that everything fails to exist at *that* time. Aquinas' followers and commentators have tried to mend matters by various ingenious suggestions; none of these, I believe, is successful.[4]

4. See Plantinga, *God and Other Minds*, chap. 10.

b The Teleological Argument

A classic version of the teleological argument is given by William Paley, Archdeacon of Carlisle and an eminent eighteenth-century philosopher:

In crossing a heath, suppose I pitched my foot against a *stone*, and were asked how the stone came to be there, I might possibly answer, that for any thing I knew to the contrary, it had lain there for ever: nor would it perhaps be very easy to show the absurdity of this answer. But suppose I had found a *watch* upon the ground, and it should be inquired how the watch happened to be in that place, I should hardly think of the answer which I had before given, that, for any thing I knew the watch might have always been there. Yet why should not this answer serve for the watch, as well as for the stone? Why is it not as admissible in the second case, as in the first? For this reason, and for no other, viz., that, when we come to inspect the watch, we perceive (what we could not discover in the stone) that its several parts are framed and put together for a purpose, e.g., that they are so formed and adjusted as to produce motion, and that motion so regulated as to point out the hour of the day; that, if the several parts had been differently shaped from what they are, of a different size from what they are, or placed after any other manner, or in any other order, then that in which they are placed, either no motion at all would have been carried on in the machine, or none which would have answered the use that is now served by it.[5]

5. William Paley, *Natural Theology*, ed. Frederick Ferre (New York: Bobbs-Merrill, Co., Inc., 1963), p. 1.

Paley goes on to claim that the universe resembles a watch in that it gives the appearance of having been designed to accomplish certain purposes; so, he says, we must conclude that the universe actually was designed by a very powerful and wise being.

David Hume states, but does not himself accept, a similar version in his *Dialogues Concerning Natural Religion*—a work that is nearly matchless for imagination and stylistic grace:

> Look round the world: contemplate the whole and every part of it: you will find it to be nothing but one great machine, subdivided into an infinite number of lesser machines, which again admit of subdivisions, to a degree beyond what human faculties can trace and explain. All these various machines, and even their most minute parts, are adjusted to each other with an accuracy, which ravishes into admiration all men, who have ever contemplated them. The curious adapting of means to ends, throughout all nature, resembles exactly, though it much exceeds, the productions of human contrivance; of human design, thought, wisdom and intelligence. Since therefore the effects resemble one another, we are led to infer, by all the rules of analogy, that the causes also resemble; and that the author of nature is somewhat similar to the mind of man; though possessed of much larger faculties, proportioned to the grandeur of the work, which he has executed.[6]

Most of Hume's *Dialogues* is devoted to criticism of the argument. For example:

> But were this world ever so perfect a production, it must still remain uncertain whether all the excellences of the work can justly be ascribed to the workman. If we survey a ship, what an exalted idea must we form of the ingenuity of the carpenter who framed so complicated, useful, and beautiful a machine? And what surprise must we feel when we find him a stupid mechanic who imitated others, and copied an art which, through a long succession of ages, after multiplied trials, mistakes, corrections, deliberations, and controversies, had been gradually improved? Many worlds might have been botched and bungled, throughout an eternity, ere this system was struck out; much labor lost; many fruitless trials made; and

6. Hume, *Dialogues Concerning Natural Religion*, p. 22.

a slow but continued improvement carried on during infinite ages in the art of world-making. In such subjects, who can determine where the truth, nay, who can conjecture where the probability lies, amidst a great number of hypotheses which may be proposed, and a still greater which may be imagined?

And what shadow of an argument, continued Philo, can you produce from your hypothesis to prove the unity of the Deity? A great number of men join in building a house or ship, in rearing a city, in framing a commonwealth; why may not several deities combine in contriving and framing a world? This is only so much greater similarity to human affairs. By sharing the work among several, we may so much further limit the attributes of each, and get rid of that extensive power and knowledge which must be supposed in one deity, and which, according to you, can only serve to weaken the proof of his existence. And if such foolish, such vicious creatures as man can yet often unite in framing and executing one plan, how much more those deities or demons, whom we may suppose several degrees more perfect?[7]

Hume's criticism, essentially, is that the evidence to which the teleological argument directs our attention supports only a *part* of theistic belief; with respect to the other parts it is quite ambiguous. That the universe is designed is a part of theistic belief, and the teleological argument perhaps gives us some (though not very much) evidence for that. But it gives us no evidence at all for the rest of what is essential to theism.

Perhaps we can spell this out a bit more fully. In believing that God exists, the theist believes a proposition logically equivalent to a *conjunction;* among the conjuncts we should find at least the following:

(1) The universe was designed
(2) The universe was designed by exactly one person
(3) The universe was created *ex nihilo* ⟶ nothing is created from nothing.
(4) The universe was created by the person who designed it

7. Ibid., pp. 51–52.

(5) The creator of the universe is omniscient, omnipotent, and perfectly good

and

(6) The creator of the universe is an eternal spirit, without body, and in no way dependent upon physical objects.

Now we can put the objection as follows. Perhaps the teleological argument gives us a smidgin of evidence for (1); but it does nothing at all for (2) through (6). The sort of evidence to which it directs our attention is entirely ambiguous with respect to these others. Consider (2) for example. We know of many large, complicated things that have been designed by one person; but just as often something of this sort is the product of a joint effort. Perhaps, Philo suggests, the universe was designed by a *committee* of deities of some sort. (Or perhaps it is the first unsteady attempt of an infant deity, or the last feeble effort of a superannuated one.) The point is that on our evidence a proposition inconsistent with (2) is just as probable as is (2) itself; but then it follows that (2) is not more probable than not on our evidence. The same comment holds for (3) through (6). Consider the conjunction of (4) with (6), says Philo: our evidence affords an argument *against* it in that every intelligent person we know about has had a body; so probably all intelligent persons have bodies, in which case the designer-creator of the universe does too. In the same way we may argue that he is dependent upon physical objects in various ways, and had parents.

Hume's criticism seems correct. The conclusion to be drawn, I think, is that the teleological argument, like the cosmological, is unsuccessful.[8]

8. For a fuller discussion of this argument see Plantinga, *God and Other Minds*, chap. 4.

c The Ontological Argument

The third theistic argument I wish to discuss is the famous "ontological argument" first formulated by Anselm of Canterbury in the eleventh century. This argument for the existence of God has fascinated philosophers ever since Anselm first stated it. Few people, I should think, have been brought to belief in God by means of this argument; nor has it played much of a role in strengthening and confirming religious faith. At first sight Anselm's argument is remarkably unconvincing if not downright irritating; it looks too much like a parlor puzzle or word magic. And yet nearly every major philosopher from the time of Anselm to the present has had something to say about it; this argument has a long and illustrious line of defenders extending to the present. Indeed, the last few years have seen a remarkable flurry of interest in it among philosophers. What accounts for its fascination? Not, I think, its religious significance, although that can be underrated. Perhaps there are two reasons for it. First, many of the most knotty and difficult problems in philosophy meet in this argument. Is existence a property? Are existential propositions—propositions of the form x *exists*—ever necessarily true? Are existential propositions about what they seem to be about? Are there, in any respectable sense of "are," some objects that do not exist? If so, do they have any properties? Can they be compared with things that do exist? These issues and a hundred others arise in connection with Anselm's argument. And second, although the argument certainly looks at first sight as if it ought to be unsound, it is profoundly difficult to say what, exactly, is wrong with it. Indeed, I do not believe that any philosopher has ever given a cogent and conclusive refutation of the ontological argument in its various forms.

Anselm states his argument as follows:

> And so, Lord, do thou, who dost give understanding to faith, give me, so far as thou knowest it to be profitable, to understand that thou art as we believe; and that thou art that which we believe. And indeed, we believe that thou art a being than which nothing greater can be conceived. Or is there no such nature, since the fool hath said in his heart, there is no God? . . . But, at any rate, this very fool when he hears of this being of which I speak—a being than which nothing greater can be conceived—understands what he hears, and what he understands is in his understanding, although he does not understand it to exist.
>
> For, it is one thing for any object to be in the understanding, and another to understand that the object exists. When a painter first conceives of what he will afterwards perform, he has it in his understanding, but he does not yet understand it to be, because he has not yet performed it. But after he has made the painting, he both has it in his understanding, and he understands that it exists, because he has made it.
>
> Hence, even the fool is convinced that something exists in the understanding, at least, than which nothing greater can be conceived. For when he hears of this, he understands it. And whatever is understood, exists in the understanding. And assuredly that, than which nothing greater can be conceived, cannot exist in the understanding alone. For, suppose it exists in the understanding alone; then it can be conceived to exist in reality; which is greater.
>
> Therefore, if that, than which nothing greater can be conceived, exists in the understanding alone, the very being, than which nothing greater can be conceived, is one, than which a greater can be conceived. But obviously this is impossible. Hence, there is no doubt that there exists a being, than which nothing greater can be conceived, and it exists both in the understanding and in reality.[9]

9. St. Anselm, *Proslogium*, chap. 2, in *The Ontological Argument*, ed. A. Plantinga (New York: Doubleday Anchor, 1965), pp. 3–4.

At first sight, this argument smacks of trumpery and deceit; but suppose we look at it a bit more closely. Its essentials are contained in these words:

> And assuredly that, than which nothing greater can be conceived, cannot exist in the understanding alone. For suppose it exists in the understanding alone; then it can be conceived to exist in reality; which is greater.

> Therefore, if that, than which nothing greater can be conceived, exists in the understanding alone, the very being, than which nothing greater can be conceived, is one, than which a greater can be conceived. But obviously this is impossible. Hence there is no doubt that there exists a being, than which nothing greater can be conceived, and it exists both in the understanding and in reality.[10]

How can we outline this argument? It is best construed, I think, as a *reductio ad absurdum* argument. In a *reductio* you prove a given proposition *p* by showing that its denial, *not-p*, leads to (or more strictly, entails) a contradiction or some other kind of absurdity. Anselm's argument can be seen as an attempt to deduce an absurdity from the proposition that there is no God. If we use the term "God" as an abbreviation for Anselm's phrase "the being than which nothing greater can be conceived," then the argument seems to go approximately as follows: Suppose

(1) God exists in the understanding but not in reality.
(2) Existence in reality is greater than existence in the understanding alone. (premise) *better to really exist than to be in someone's imagination.*
(3) God's existence in reality is conceivable. (premise)
(4) If God did exist in reality, then He would be greater than He is. [from (1) and (2)]
(5) It is conceivable that there is a being greater than God is. [(3) and (4)]
(6) It is conceivable that there be a being greater than the being than which nothing greater can be conceived. [(5) by the definition of "God"]

10. Ibid., pp. 4.

But surely (6) is absurd and self-contradictory; how could we conceive of a being greater than the being than which none greater can be conceived? So we may conclude that

(7) It is false that God exists in the understanding but not in reality

It follows that if God exists in the understanding, He also exists in reality; but clearly enough He *does* exist in the understanding, as even the fool will testify; therefore, He exists in reality as well.

Now when Anselm says that a being *exists in the understanding*, we may take him, I think, as saying that someone has *thought of* or thought about that being. When he says that something *exists in reality*, on the other hand, he means to say simply that the thing in question really does exist. And when he says that a certain state of affairs is *conceivable*, he means to say, I believe, that this state of affairs is possible in our broadly logical sense (see p. 15); there is a possible world in which it obtains. This means that step (3) above may be put more perspicuously as

(3') It is possible that God exists

and step (6) as

(6') It is possible that there be a being greater than the being than which it is not possible that there be a greater.

An interesting feature of this argument is that all of its premises are *necessarily* true if true at all. (1) is the assumption from which Anselm means to deduce a contradiction. (2) is a premise, and presumably necessarily true in Anselm's view; and (3) is the only remaining premise (the other items are consequences of preceding steps); it says of some *other* proposition *(God exists)* that it is possible. Propositions which thus ascribe a modality—possibility, necessity, contingency—to another proposition are themselves either necessarily true or necessarily false. So all the premises of the argument are, if true at all, necessarily true. And hence if the premises of this argument are true, then [provided that (6) is really inconsistent] a contradiction can be deduced from (1) together with necessary propositions; this means that (1) entails a contradiction and is, therefore, necessarily false.

1. Gaunilo's Objection

Gaunilo, a contemporary of Anselm's, wrote a reply which he entitled *On Behalf of the Fool.* Here is the essence of his objection.

> For example: it is said that somewhere in the ocean is an island, which, because of the difficulty, or rather the impossibility, of discovering what does not exist, is called the lost island. And they say that this island has an inestimable wealth of all manner of riches and delicacies in greater abundance than is told of the Islands of the Blest; and that having no owner or inhabitant, it is more excellent than all other countries, which are inhabited by mankind, in the abundance with which it is stored.
>
> Now if some one should tell me that there is such an island, I should easily understand his words, in which there is no difficulty. But suppose that he went on to say, as if by a logical inference: "You can no longer doubt that this island which is more excellent than all lands exists somewhere, since you have no doubt that it is in your understanding. And since it is more excellent not to be in the understanding alone, but to exist both in the understanding and in reality, for this reason it must exist. For if it does not exist, any land which really exists will be more excellent than it; and so the island already understood by you to be more excellent will not be more excellent."
>
> If a man should try to prove to me by such reasoning that this island truly exists, and that its existence should no longer be doubted, either I should believe that he was jesting, or I know not which I ought to regard as the greater fool: myself, supposing that I should allow this proof; or him, if he should suppose that he had established with any certainty the existence of this island.[11]

Gaunilo was the first of many to try to discredit the ontological argument by showing that one can find similar arguments to prove the existence of all sorts of absurd things—a greatest possible island, a highest possible mountain, a greatest possible middle linebacker, a

11. Plantinga, *The Ontological Argument,* p. 11.

meanest possible man, and the like. But Anselm was not without a reply.[12]

He points out, first, that Gaunilo misquotes him. What is under consideration is not a being that is *in fact* greater than any other, but one such that a greater *cannot be conceived;* a being than which it's *not possible* that there be a greater. Gaunilo seems to overlook this. And thus his famous lost island argument isn't strictly parallel to Anselm's argument; his conclusion should be only that there is an island such that no other island is greater than it—which, if there are any islands at all, is a fairly innocuous conclusion.

But obviously Gaunilo's argument can be revised. Instead of speaking, as he did, of an island that is more excellent than all others, let's speak instead of an island than which a greater or more excellent cannot be conceived—an island, that is, than which it's not possible that there be a greater. Couldn't we use an argument like Anselm's to "establish" the existence of such an island, and if we could, wouldn't that show that Anselm's argument is fallacious?

2. Anselm's Reply

Not obviously. Anselm's proper reply, it seems to me, is that it's impossible that there be such an island. The idea of an island than which it's not possible that there be a greater is like the idea of a natural number than which it's not possible that there be a greater, or the idea of a line than which none more crooked is possible. There neither is nor could be a greatest possible natural number; indeed, there isn't a greatest *actual* number, let alone a greatest possible. And the same goes for islands. No matter how great an island is, no matter how many Nubian maidens and dancing girls adorn it, there could always be a greater—

12. Ibid., pp. 13–27.

one with twice as many, for example. The qualities that make for greatness in islands—number of palm trees, amount and quality of coconuts, for example—most of these qualities have no *intrinsic maximum*. That is, there is no degree of productivity or number of palm trees (or of dancing girls) such that it is impossible that an island display more of that quality. So the idea of a greatest possible island is an inconsistent or incoherent idea; it's not possible that there be such a thing. And hence the analogue of step (3) of Anselm's argument (it is possible that God exists) is not true for the perfect island argument; so that argument fails.

But doesn't Anselm's argument itself founder upon the same rock? If the idea of a greatest possible island is inconsistent, won't the same hold for the idea of a greatest possible being? Perhaps not. For what are the properties in virtue of which one being is greater, just as a being, than another? Anselm clearly has in mind such properties as wisdom, knowledge, power, and moral excellence or moral perfection. And certainly knowledge, for example, does have an intrinsic maximum: if for every proposition p, a being B knows whether or not p is true, then B has a degree of knowledge that is utterly unsurpassable. So a greatest possible being would have to have this kind of knowledge: it would have to be *omniscient*. Similarly for *power;* omnipotence is a degree of power that can't possibly be excelled. Moral perfection or moral excellence is perhaps not quite so clear; still a being could perhaps always do what is morally right, so that it would not be possible for it to be exceeded along those lines. But what about a quality like *love?* Wouldn't that be a property that makes for greatness? God, according to Christian theism, loves His children and demonstrated His love in the redemptive events of the life and death of Jesus Christ. And what about the relevant qualities here—love, or acting out of love: do they have intrinsic maxima? The answer isn't very clear either way. Rather than pause to discuss this question, let's note simply that there may be a weak point here in Anselm's argument and move on.

3.   Kant's Objection

The most famous and important objection to the ontological argument is contained in Immanuel Kant's *Critique of Pure Reason*.[13] Kant begins his criticism as follows:

> If, in an identical proposition, I reject the predicate while retaining the subject, contradiction results; and I therefore say that the former belongs necessarily to the latter. But if we reject the subject and predicate alike, there is no contradiction; for nothing is then left that can be contradicted. To posit a triangle, and yet to reject its three angles, is self-contradictory; but there is no contradiction in rejecting the triangle together with its three angles. The same holds true of the concept of an absolutely necessary being. If its existence is rejected, we reject the thing itself with all its predicates; and no question of contradiction can then arise. There is nothing outside it that would then be contradicted, since the necessity of the thing is not supposed to be derived from anything external; nor is there anything internal that would be contradicted, since in rejecting the thing itself we have at the same time rejected all its internal properties. "God is omnipotent" is a necessary judgment. The omnipotence cannot be rejected if we posit a Deity, that is, an infinite being; for the two concepts are identical. But if we say "There is no God," neither the omnipotence nor any other of its predicates is given; they are one and all rejected together with the subject, and there is therefore not the least contradiction in such a judgment. . . .
>
> For I cannot form the least concept of a thing which, should it be rejected with all its predicates, leaves behind a contradiction.[14]

One characteristic feature of Anselm's argument, as we have seen, is that if successful, it establishes that *God exists* is a *necessary* proposition. Here Kant is apparently arguing that no *existential* proposition—one

13. Immanuel Kant, *Critique of Pure Reason*, ed. Norman Kemp Smith (New York: Macmillan Co., 1929). Some relevant passages are reprinted in Plantinga, *The Ontological Argument*, pp. 57–64.

14. Plantinga, *The Ontological Argument*, p. 59.

that asserts the existence of something or other—is necessarily true; the reason, he says, is that no *contra-existential* (the denial of an existential) is contradictory or inconsistent. But in which of our several senses of inconsistent? What he means to say, I believe, is that no existential proposition is necessary in the broadly logical sense. And this claim has been popular with philosophers ever since. But why, exactly, does Kant think it's true? What is the argument? When we take a careful look at the purported reasoning, it looks pretty unimpressive; it's hard to make out an argument at all. The conclusion would apparently be this: if we deny the existence of something or other, we can't be contradicting ourselves; no existential proposition is necessary and no contra-existential is impossible. Why not? Well, if we say, for example, that God does not exist, then says Kant, "There is nothing outside it (i.e., God) that would then be contradicted, since the necessity of the thing is not supposed to be derived from anything external; nor is there anything internal that would be contradicted, since in rejecting the thing itself we have at the same time rejected all its internal properties."

But how is this even *relevant?* The claim is that *God does not exist* can't be necessarily false. What could be meant, in this context, by saying that there's nothing "outside of" God that would be contradicted if we denied His existence? What would contradict a proposition like *God does not exist* is some other proposition—*God does exist*, for example. Kant seems to think that if the proposition in question *were* necessarily false, it would have to contradict, not a proposition, but some *object* external to God—or else contradict some internal part or aspect or property of God. But this certainly looks like confusion; it is *propositions* that contradict each other; they aren't contradicted by objects or parts, aspects or properties of objects. Does he mean instead to be speaking of *propositions* about things external to God, or about his aspects or parts or properties? But clearly many such propositions do contradict *God does not exist;* an example would be *the world was created by God.* Does he mean to say that no *true* proposition contradicts *God does not exist?* No, for that would be to affirm the *nonexistence* of God, an affirmation Kant is by no means prepared to make.

So this passage is an enigma. Either Kant was confused or else he expressed himself very badly indeed. And either way we don't have any argument for the claim that contra-existential propositions can't be inconsistent. This passage seems to be no more than an elaborate and confused way of *asserting* this claim.

The heart of Kant's objection to the ontological argument, however, is contained in the following passage:

"Being" is obviously not a real predicate; that is, it is not a concept of something which could be added to the concept of a thing. It is merely the positing of a thing, or of certain determinations, as existing in themselves. Logically, it is merely the copula of a judgment. The proposition "God is omnipotent" contains two concepts, each of which has its object—God and omnipotence. The small word "is" adds no new predicate, but only serves to posit the predicate in its relation to the subject. If, now, we take the subject (God) with all its predicates (among which is omnipotence), and say "God is," or "There is a God," we attach no new predicate to the concept of God, but only posit it as an object that stands in relation to my concept. The content of both must be one and the same; nothing can have been added to the concept, which expresses merely what is possible, by my thinkings its object (through the expression "it is") as given absolutely. Otherwise stated, the real contains no more than the merely possible. A hundred real thalers not contain the least coin more than a hundred possible thalers. For as the latter signify the concept and the former the object and the positing of the concept, should the former contain more than the latter, my concept would not, in that case, express the whole object, and would not therefore be an adequate concept of it. My financial position, however, is affected very differently by a hundred real thalers than it is by the mere concept of them (that is, of the possibility). For the object, as it actually exists, is not analytically contained in my concept, but is added to my concept (which is a determination of my state) synthetically; and yet the conceived hundred thalers are not themselves in the least increased through thus acquiring existence outside my concept.

By whatever and by however many predicates we may think a thing—even if we completely determine it—we do not make the least addition to the thing when we further declare that this thing is. Otherwise it would not be exactly the same thing that exists, but something more than we had thought in the concept: and we could not, therefore, say that the object of my concept exists. If we think in a thing every feature of reality except one, the missing reality is not added by my saying that this defective thing exists.[15]

Now how, exactly is all this relevant to Anselm's argument? Perhaps Kant means to make a point that we could put by saying that it's not possible to *define things into existence.* (People sometimes suggest that the ontological argument is just such an attempt to define *God* into existence.) And this claim is somehow connected with Kant's famous but perplexing *dictum* that *being* (or existence) is not a real predicate or property. But how shall we understand Kant here? What does it mean to say that existence isn't (or is) a real property?

Apparently Kant thinks this is equivalent to or follows from what he puts variously as "the real *contains* no more than the merely possible"; "the *content* of both (i.e., concept and object) must be one and the same"; "being is not the concept of something that could be *added to* the concept of a thing," and so on. But what does all this mean? And how does it bear on the ontological argument? Perhaps Kant is thinking along the following lines. In defining a concept—*bachelor,* let's say, or *prime number*—one lists a number of properties that are *severally necessary* and *jointly sufficient* for the concept's applying to something. That is, the concept applies to a given thing only if that thing has each of the listed properties, and if a thing does have them all, then the concept in question applies to it. So, for example, to define the concept *bachelor* we list such properties as *being unmarried, being male, being over the age of twenty-five,* and the like. Take any one of these properties: a thing is a bachelor only if it has it, and if a thing has all of them, then it follows that it is a bachelor.

Now suppose you have a concept *C* that has application *contingently* if at all. That is to say, it is not necessarily true that there are things to which this concept applies. The concept *bachelor* would be an example; the proposition *there are bachelors,* while *true,* is obviously not necessarily true. And suppose $P_1, P_2 \ldots, P_n$ are the properties jointly sufficient

15. Ibid., pp. 61–62.

and severally necessary for something's falling under C. Then C can be defined as follows:

> A thing x is an instance of C (i.e., C applies to x) if and only if x has $P_1, P_2 \ldots, P_n$.

Perhaps Kant's point is this. There is a certain kind of mistake here we may be tempted to make. Suppose $P_1, \ldots, P_n$ are the defining properties for the concept *bachelor*. We might try to define a new concept *superbachelor* by adding *existence* to $P_1, \ldots, P_n$. That is, we might say

> x is a superbachelor if and only if x has $P_1, P_2, \ldots, P_n$, and x exists.

Then (as we might mistakenly suppose) just as it is a necessary truth that bachelors are unmarried, so it is a necessary truth that superbachelors exist. And in this way it looks as if we've defined superbachelors into existence.

But of course this is a mistake, and perhaps that is Kant's point. For while indeed it is a necessary truth that bachelors are unmarried, what this means is that the proposition

> (8) Everything that is a bachelor is unmarried

is necessarily true. Similarly, then,

> (9) Everything that is a superbachelor exists

will be necessarily true. But obviously it doesn't follow that there *are* any superbachelors. All that follows is that

> (10) All the superbachelors there are *exist*

which is not really very startling. If it is a contingent truth, furthermore, that there are bachelors, it will be equally contingent that there are superbachelors. We can see this by noting that the defining properties of the concept *bachelor* are included among those of *superbachelor;* it is a necessary truth, therefore, that every superbachelor is a bachelor. This means that

(11) There are some superbachelors

entails

(12) There are some bachelors.

But then if (12) is contingent, so is (11). Indeed, the concepts *bachelor* and *superbachelor* are equivalent in the following sense: it is impossible that there exists an object to which one but not the other of these two concepts applies. We've just seen that every superbachelor must be a bachelor. Conversely, however, every bachelor is a superbachelor: for every bachelor exists and every existent bachelor is a superbachelor. Now perhaps we can put Kant's point more exactly. Suppose we say that a property or predicate P is *real* only if there is some list of properties P_1 to P_n such that the result of adding P to the list does not define a concept equivalent (in the above sense) to that defined by the list. It then follows, of course, that existence is not a real property or predicate. Kant's point, then, is that one cannot *define things into existence* because *existence* is not a real property or predicate in the explained sense.[16]

4. The Irrelevance of Kant's Objection

If this is what he means, he's certainly right. But is it relevant to the ontological argument? Couldn't Anselm thank Kant for this interesting point and proceed merrily on his way? Where did he try to define God into being by adding existence to a list of properties that defined some concept? According to the great German philosopher and pessimist Arthur Schopenhauer, the ontological argument arises when "someone excogitates a conception, composed out of all sorts of predicates, among

16. For a more detailed and extensive discussion of this argument, see Plantinga, *God and Other Minds*, pp. 29–38 and A. Plantinga, "Kant's Objection to the Ontological Argument," *Journal of Philosophy* 63 (1966): 537.

which, however, he takes care to include the predicate actuality or existence, either openly or wrapped up for decency's sake in some other predicate, such as perfection, immensity, or something of the kind." If this were Anselm's procedure—if he had simply added existence to a concept that has application contingently if at all—then indeed his argument would be subject to the Kantian criticism. But he didn't, and it isn't.

The usual criticisms of Anselm's argument, then, leave much to be desired. Of course, this doesn't mean that the argument is successful, but it does mean that we shall have to take an independent look at it. What about Anselm's argument? Is it a good one? The first thing to recognize is that the ontological argument comes in an enormous variety of versions, some of which may be much more promising than others. Instead of speaking of *the* ontological argument, we must recognize that what we have here is a whole family of related arguments. (Having said this I shall violate my own directive and continue to speak of *the* ontological argument.)

5.　The Argument Restated

Let's look once again at our initial schematization of the argument. I think perhaps it is step (2)

(2) Existence in reality is greater than existence in the understanding alone

that is most puzzling here. Earlier we spoke of the properties in virtue of which one being is greater, just as a being, than another. Suppose we call them *great-making properties*. Apparently Anselm means to suggest that *existence* is a great-making property. He seems to suggest that a nonexistent being would be greater than in fact it is, if it did exist. But how can we make sense of that? How could there be a nonexistent being anyway? Does that so much as make sense?

being clearly expressed

Perhaps we can put this perspicuously in terms of possible worlds. You recall that an object may exist in some possible worlds and not others. There are possible worlds in which you and I do not exist; these worlds are impoverished, no doubt, but are not on that account impossible. Furthermore, you recall that an object can have different properties in different worlds. In the actual world Paul J. Zwier is not a good tennis player; but surely there are worlds in which he wins the Wimbledon Open. Now if a person can have different properties in different worlds, then he can have different degrees of greatness in different worlds. In the actual world Raquel Welch has impressive assets; but there is a world RW_f in which she is fifty pounds overweight and mousy. Indeed, there are worlds in which she does not so much as exist. What Anselm means to be suggesting, I think, is that Raquel Welch enjoys very little greatness in those worlds in which she does not exist. But of course this condition is not restricted to Miss Welch. What Anselm means to say, more generally, is that for any being x and worlds W and W', if x exists in W but not in W', then x's greatness in W exceeds x's greatness in W'. Or, more modestly, perhaps he means to say that if a being x does not exist in a world W (and there is a world in which x does exist), then *there is at least one world* in which the greatness of x exceeds the greatness of x in W. Suppose Raquel Welch does not exist in some world W. Anselm means to say that there is at least one possible world in which she has a degree of greatness that exceeds the degree of greatness she has in that world W. (It is plausible, indeed, to go much further and hold that she has *no greatness at all* in worlds in which she does not exist.)

But now perhaps we can restate the whole argument in a way that gives us more insight into its real structure. Once more, use the term "God" to abbreviate the phrase "the being than which it is not possible that there be a greater." Now suppose

(13) God does not exist in the actual world

Add the new version of premise (2):

(14) For any being x and world W, if x does not exist in W, then there
is a world W' such that the greatness of x in W' exceeds the greatness
of x in W.

Restate premise (3) in terms of possible worlds:

(15) There is a possible world in which God exists.

And continue on:

(16) If God does not exist in the actual world, then there is a world
W' such that the greatness of God in W' exceeds the greatness of God
in the actual world. [from (14)]

(17) So there is a world W' such that the greatness of God in W'
exceeds the greatness of God in the actual world. [(13) and (16)]

(18) So there is a possible being x and a world W' such that the greatness
of x in W' exceeds the greatness of God in actuality. [(17)]

(19) Hence it's possible that there be a being greater than God is. [(18)]

(20) So it's possible that there be a being greater than the being than
which it's not possible that there be a greater. (19), replacing "God" by
what it abbreviates

But surely

(21) It's not possible that there be a being greater than the being than
which it's not possible that there be a greater.

So (13) [with the help of premises (14) and (15)] appears to imply (20),
which, according to (21), is necessarily false. Accordingly, (13) is false.
So the actual world contains a being than which it's not possible that
there be a greater—that is, God exists.

Now where, if anywhere, can we fault this argument? Step (13) is the
hypothesis for *reductio*, the assumption to be reduced to absurdity, and
is thus entirely above reproach. Steps (16) through (20) certainly look
as if they follow from the items they are said to follow from. So that
leaves only (14), (15), and (20). Step (14) says only that it is possible that
God exists. Step (15) also certainly seems plausible: if a being doesn't
even *exist* in a given world, it can't have much by way of greatness in
that world. At the very least it can't have its *maximum* degree of
greatness—a degree of greatness that it does not excel in any other world
—in a world where it doesn't exist. And consider (20): surely it has the

ring of truth. How could there be a being greater than the being than which it's not possible that there be a greater? Initially, the argument seems pretty formidable.

6. Its Fatal Flaw

But there is something puzzling about it. We can see this if we ask what sorts of things (14) is supposed to be *about*. It starts off boldly: "For any being x and world W, . . ." So (14) is talking about worlds and beings. It says something about each world-being pair. And (16) follows from it, because (16) asserts of *God* and *the actual world* something that according to (14) holds of every being and world. But then if (16) follows from (14), God must be a *being*. That is, (16) follows from (14) only with the help of the additional premise that God is a being. And doesn't this statement—that God is a being—imply that *there is* or *exists* a being than which it's not possible that there be a greater? But if so, the argument flagrantly begs the question; for then we can accept the inference from (14) to (16) only if we already know that the conclusion is true.

We can approach this same matter by a slightly different route. I asked earlier what sorts of things (14) was *about;* the answer was: beings and worlds. We can ask the same or nearly the same question by asking about the *range* of the *quantifiers*—"for any being," "for any world"— in (14). What do these quantifiers range over? If we reply that they range over possible worlds and beings—*actually existing* beings—then the inference to (16) requires the additional premise that God is an actually existing being, that there *really is* a being than which it is not possible that there be a greater. Since this is supposed to be our conclusion, we can't very gracefully add it as a *premise.* So perhaps the quantifiers don't range just over actually existing beings. But what else is there? Step (18) speaks of a *possible being*—a thing that may not in fact exist, but *could* exist. Or we could put it like this. A possible being is a thing that exists in some possible world or other; a thing x for which there is a world W, such that if W had been actual, x would have existed. So (18) is really about worlds and *possible beings*. And what it says is this: take any possible being x and any possible world W. If x does not exist in W, then there is a possible world W' where x has a degree of greatness that surpasses the greatness that it has in W. And hence to make the argument complete perhaps we should add the affirmation that God is a *possible being*.

But *are* there any possible beings—that is, *merely* possible beings, beings that don't in fact exist? If so, what sorts of things are they? Do they have properties? How are we to think of them? What is their status? And what reasons are there for supposing that there are any such peculiar items at all?

These are knotty problems. Must we settle them in order even to consider this argument? No. For instead of speaking of *possible beings* and the worlds in which they do or don't exist, we can speak of *properties* and the worlds in which they do or don't *have instances*, are or are not *instantiated* or *exemplified*. Instead of speaking of a possible being named by the phrase, "the being than which it's not possible that there be a greater," we may speak of the property *having an unsurpassable degree of greatness*—that is, *having a degree of greatness such that it's not possible that there exist a being having more*. And then we can ask whether this property is instantiated in this or other possible worlds. Later on I shall show how to restate the argument this way. For the moment please take my word for the fact that we can speak as freely as we wish about possible objects; for we can always translate ostensible talk about such things into talk about properties and the worlds in which they are or are not instantiated.

The argument speaks, therefore, of an unsurpassably great being—of a being whose greatness is not excelled by any being in any world. This being has a degree of greatness so impressive that no other being in any world has more. But here we hit the question crucial for this version of the argument. *Where* does this being have that degree of greatness? I said above that the same being may have different degrees of greatness in different worlds; in which world does the possible being in question have the degree of greatness in question? All we are really told, in being told that God is a possible being, is this: among the possible beings there is one that in some world or other has a degree of greatness that is nowhere excelled.

And this fact is fatal to this version of the argument. I said earlier that (21) has the ring of truth; a closer look (listen?) reveals that it's more of a dull thud. For it is ambiguous as between

(21') It's not possible that there be a being whose greatness surpasses that enjoyed by the unsurpassably great being *in the worlds where its greatness is at a maximum*

and

(21") It's not possible that there be a being whose greatness surpasses that enjoyed by the unsurpassably great being *in the actual world.*

There is an important difference between these two. The greatest possible being may have different degrees of greatness in different worlds. Step (21') points to the worlds in which this being has its maximal greatness; and it says, quite properly, that the degree of greatness this being has in those worlds is nowhere excelled. Clearly this is so. The greatest possible being is a possible being who in some world or other has unsurpassable greatness. Unfortunately for the argument, however, (21') does not contradict (20). Or to put it another way, what follows from (13) [together with (14) and (15)] is not the denial of (21'). If that *did* follow, then the *reductio* would be complete and the argument successful. But what (20) says is not that there is a possible being whose greatness exceeds that enjoyed by the greatest possible being *in a world where the latter's greatness is at a maximum;* it says only that there is a possible being whose greatness exceeds that enjoyed by the greatest possible being *in the actual world*—where, for all we know, its greatness is *not* at a maximum. So if we read (21) as (21'), the *reductio* argument falls apart.

Suppose instead we read it as (21"). Then what it says is that there couldn't be a being whose greatness surpasses that enjoyed by the greatest possible being in Kronos, the actual world. So read, (21) does contradict (20). Unfortunately, however, we have no reason, so far, for thinking that (21") is true at all, let alone necessarily true. If, among the possible beings, there is one whose greatness *in some world or other* is absolutely maximal—such that no being in any world has a degree of greatness surpassing it—then indeed there couldn't be a being that was greater than *that*. But it doesn't follow that this being has that degree of greatness in the *actual* world. It has it *in some world or other* but not necessarily in Kronos, the actual world. And so the argument fails. If we take (21) as (21'), then it follows from the assertion that God is a possible being; but it is of no use to the argument. If we take it as (21"), on the other hand, then indeed it is useful in the argument, but we have no reason whatever to think it true. So this version of the argument fails.[17]

7. A Modal Version of the Argument

But of course there are many other versions; one of the argument's chief features is its many-sided diversity. The fact that *this* version is unsatisfactory does not show that *every* version is or must be. Professors Charles Hartshorne[18] and Norman Malcolm[19] claim to detect two quite different versions of the argument in Anselm's work. In the first of these versions *existence* is held to be a perfection or a great-making property; in the second it is *necessary existence*. But what could *that* amount to? Perhaps something like this. Consider a pair of beings A and B that both

17. This criticism of this version of the argument essentially follows David Lewis, "Anselm and Actuality," *Nous* 4 (1970): 175–188. See also Plantinga, *The Nature of Necessity*, pp. 202–205.

18. Charles Hartshorne, *Man's Vision of God* (New York: Harper and Row, 1941). Portions reprinted in Plantinga, *The Ontological Argument*, pp. 123–135.

19. Norman Malcolm, "Anselm's Ontological Arguments," *Philosophical Review* 69 (1960); reprinted in Plantinga, *The Ontological Argument*, pp. 136–159.

do in fact exist. And suppose that A exists in every other possible world as well—that is, if any other possible world has been actual, A would have existed. On the other hand, B exists in only some possible worlds; there are worlds W such that had any of *them* been actual, B would not have existed. Now according to the doctrine under consideration, A is so far greater than B. Of course, *on balance* it may be that A is not greater than B; I believe that the number seven, unlike Spiro Agnew, exists in every possible world; yet I should be hesitant to affirm on that account that the number seven is greater than Agnew. Necessary existence is just one of several great-making properties, and no doubt Agnew has more of some of these others than does the number seven. Still, all this is compatible with saying that necessary existence is a great-making property. And given this notion, we can restate the argument as follows:

(22) It is possible that there is a greatest possible being.

(23) Therefore, there is a possible being that in some world W' or other has a maximum degree of greatness—a degree of greatness that is nowhere exceeded.

(24) A being B has the maximum degree of greatness in a given possible world W only if B exists in every possible world.

(22) and (24) are the premises of this argument; and what follows is that if W' had been actual, B would have existed in every possible world. That is, if W' had been actual, b's nonexistence would have been impossible. But logical possibilities and impossibilities do not vary from world to world. That is to say, if a given proposition or state of affairs is impossible in at least one possible world, then it is impossible in every possible world. There are no propositions that in fact are possible but could have been impossible; there are none that are in fact impossible but could have been possible.[20] Accordingly, B's

20. See Plantinga, "World and Essence," *Philosophical Review* 79 (October 1970): 475; and Plantinga, *The Nature of Necessity*, chap. 4, sec. 6.

nonexistence is impossible in every possible world; hence it is impossible in *this* world; hence *B* exists and exists necessarily.

8.   A Flaw in the Ointment

This is an interesting argument, but it suffers from at least one annoying defect. What it shows is that if it is possible that there be a greatest possible being (if the idea of a greatest possible being is coherent) and if that idea includes necessary existence, then in fact there is a being that exists in every world and in *some* world has a degree of greatness that is nowhere excelled. Unfortunately it doesn't follow that the being in question has the degree of greatness in question in Kronos, the actual world. For all the argument shows, this being might *exist* in the actual world but be pretty insignificant here. In some world or other it has maximal greatness; how does this show that it has such greatness in Kronos?

But perhaps we can repair the argument. J. N. Findlay once offered what can only be called an ontological *disproof* of the existence of God.[21] Findlay begins by pointing out that God, if He exists, is an "adequate object of religious worship." But such a being, he says, would have to be a *necessary* being; and, he adds, this idea is incredible "for all who share a contemporary outlook." "Those who believe in necessary truths which aren't merely tautological think that such truths merely connect the *possible* instances of various characteristics with each other; they don't expect such truths to tell them whether there *will* be instances of any characteristics. This is the outcome of the whole medieval and Kantian criticism of the ontological proof."[22] I've argued above that "the whole medieval and Kantian criticism" of Anselm's argument

21. J. N. Findlay, "Can God's Existence Be Disproved?" *Mind* 57 (1948): 176–183. Reprinted in ed., Plantinga, *The Ontological Argument*, pp. 111–122.

22. P. 119. Mr. Findlay no longer endorses this sentiment. See the preface to his *Ascent to the Absolute* (1970).

may be taken with a grain or two of salt. And certainly most philosophers who believe that there are necessary truths, believe that *some* of them *do* tell us whether there will be instances of certain characteristics; the proposition *there are no married bachelors* is necessarily true, and it tells us that there will be no instances whatever of the characteristic *married bachelor*. Be that as it may what is presently relevant in Findlay's piece is this passage:

> Not only is it contrary to the demands and claims inherent in religious attitudes that their object should *exist* "accidentally"; it is also contrary to these demands that it should *possess its various excellences* in some merely adventitious manner. It would be quite unsatisfactory from the religious stand point, if an object merely *happened* to be wise, good, powerful, and so forth, even to a superlative degree. . . . And so we are led on irresistibly, by the demands inherent in religious reverence, to hold that an adequate object of our worship must possess its various excellences *in some necessary manner*.[23]

I think there is truth in these remarks. We could put the point as follows. In determining the greatness of a being B in a world W, what counts is not merely the qualities and properties possessed by B *in* W; what B is like in *other* worlds is also relevant. Most of us who believe in God think of Him as a being than whom it's not possible that there be a greater. But we don't think of Him as a being who, had things been different, would have been powerless or uninformed or of dubious moral character. God doesn't *just happen* to be a greatest possible being; He couldn't have been otherwise.

Perhaps we should make a distinction here between *greatness* and *excellence*. A being's excellence in a given world W, let us say, depends only upon the properties it has in W; its *greatness* in W depends upon these properties but also upon what it is like in other worlds. Those who are fond of the calculus might put it by saying that there is a function assigning to each being in each world a degree of excellence; and a being's *greatness* is to be computed (by someone unusually well in-

23. J. N. Findlay, "Can God's Existence Be Disproved?" p. 117.

formed) by integrating its excellence over all possible worlds. Then it is plausible to suppose that the maximal degree of greatness entails *maximal excellence in every world*. A being, then, has the maximal degree of *greatness* in a given world *W* only if it has *maximal excellence in every possible world*. But *maximal excellence* entails *omniscience, omnipotence,* and *moral perfection*. That is to say, a being *B* has maximal excellence in a world *W* only if *B* has omniscience, omnipotence, and moral perfection in *W*—only if *B* would have been omniscient, omnipotent, and morally perfect if *W* had been actual.

9. The Argument Restated

Given these ideas, we can restate the present version of the argument in the following more explicit way.

> (25) It is possible that there be a being that has maximal greatness.
> (26) So there is a possible being that in some world *W* has maximal greatness.
> (27) A Being has maximal greatness in a given world only if it has maximal excellence in every world.
> (28) A being has maximal excellence in a given world only if it has omniscience, omnipotence, and moral perfection in that world.

And now we no longer need the supposition that necessary existence is a perfection; for obviously a being can't be omnipotent (or for that matter omniscient or morally perfect) in a given world unless it *exists* in that world. From (25), (27), and (28) it follows that there actually exists a being that is omnipotent, omniscient, and morally perfect; this being, furthermore, exists and has these qualities in every other world as well. For (26), which follows from (25), tells us that there is a possible world *W'*, let's say, in which there exists a being with maximal greatness. That is, had *W'* been actual, there would have been a being with maximal greatness. But then according to (27) this being has maximal excellence in every world. What this means, according to (28), is that in W′ this being has omniscience, omnipotence, and moral perfection *in every world*. That is to say, if W′ had been actual, there would have existed a being who was omniscient and omnipotent and morally perfect and who would have had these properties in every possible world. So if W′ had been actual, it would have been *impossible* that there be no omnipotent, omniscient, and morally perfect being. But (see above, p. 88) while *contingent* truths vary from world to world, what is logically impossible does not. Therefore, in every possible world W it is impossible that there be no such being; each possible world W is such that if it had been actual, it would have been impossible that there be no such being. And hence it is impossible in the *actual* world (which is one of the possible worlds) that there be no omniscient, omnipotent, and morally perfect being. Hence there really does exist a being who is omniscient, omnipotent, and morally perfect and who exists and has these properties in every possible world. Accordingly these premises, (25), (27), and (28), entail that God, so thought of, exists. Indeed, if we regard (27) and (28) as consequences of a *definition*—a definition of maximal greatness—then the only premise of the argument is (25).

But now for a last objection suggested earlier (p. 101). What about (26)? It says that there is a *possible being* having such and such characteristics. But what *are* possible beings? We know what *actual* beings are —the Taj Mahal, Socrates, you and I, the Grand Teton—these are among the more impressive examples of actually existing beings. But what is a *possible* being? Is there a possible mountain just like Mt. Rainier two miles directly south of the Grand Teton? If so, it is located at the same place as the Middle Teton. Does that matter? Is there another such possible mountain three miles east of the Grand Teton, where Jenny Lake is? Are there possible mountains like this all over the world? Are there also possible oceans at all the places where there are possible mountains? For any place you mention, of course, it is *possible* that there be a mountain there; does it follow that in fact *there is* a possible mountain there?

These are some questions that arise when we ask ourselves whether there are merely possible beings that don't in fact exist. And the version of the ontological argument we've been considering seems to make sense only on the assumption that there are such things. The earlier versions also depended on that assumption; consider for example, this step of the first version we considered:

(18) So there is a possible being x and a world W' such that the greatness of x in W' exceeds the greatness of God in actuality.

This possible being, you recall, was God Himself, supposed not to exist in the actual world. We can make sense of (18), therefore, only if we are prepared to grant that there are possible beings who don't in fact exist. Such beings exist in other worlds, of course; had things been appropriately different, they would have existed. But in fact they don't exist, although nonetheless there *are* such things.

I am inclined to think the supposition that there are such things—things that are possible but don't in fact exist—is either unintelligible or necessarily false. But this doesn't mean that the present version of the ontological argument must be rejected. For we can restate the argument in a way that does not commit us to this questionable idea. Instead of speaking of *possible beings* that do or do not exist in various possible worlds, we may speak of *properties* and the worlds in which they are or are not *instantiated*. Instead of speaking of the possible fat man in the corner, noting that he doesn't exist, we may speak of the property *being a fat man in the corner*, noting that it isn't instantiated (although it could have been). Of course, the *property* in question, like the property *being a unicorn*, exists. It is a perfectly good property which exists with as much equanimity as the property of equininity, the property of being a horse. But it doesn't happen to apply to anything. That is, in *this* world it doesn't apply to anything; in other possible worlds it does.

10. The Argument Triumphant

Using this idea we can restate this last version of the ontological argument in such a way that it no longer matters whether there are any merely possible beings that do not exist. Instead of speaking of the possible being that has, in some world or other, a maximal degree of greatness, we may speak of *the property of being maximally great* or *maximal greatness.* The premise corresponding to (25) then says simply that maximal greatness is possibly instantiated, i.e., that

(29) There is a possible world in which maximal greatness is instantiated.

And the analogues of (27) and (28) spell out what is involved in maximal greatness:

(30) Necessarily, a being is maximally great only if it has maximal excellence in every world

and

(31) Necessarily, a being has maximal excellence in every world only if it has omniscience, omnipotence, and moral perfection in every world.

Notice that (30) and (31) do not imply that there are possible but nonexistent beings—any more than does, for example,

(32) Necessarily, a thing is a unicorn only if it has one horn.

But if (29) is true, then there is a possible world W such that if it had been actual, then there would have existed a being that was omnipotent, omniscient, and morally perfect; this being, furthermore, would have had these qualities in every possible world. So it follows that if W had been actual, it would have been *impossible* that there be no such being. That is, if W had been actual,

(33) There is no omnipotent, omniscient, and morally perfect being

would have been an impossible proposition. But if a proposition is impossible in at least one possible world, then it is impossible in every possible world; what is impossible does not vary from world to world. Accordingly (33) is impossible in the *actual* world, i.e., impossible *simpliciter*. But if it is impossible that there be no such being, then there actually exists a being that is omnipotent, omniscient, and morally perfect; this being, furthermore, has these qualities essentially and exists in every possible world.

What shall we say of this argument? It is certainly valid; given its premise, the conclusion follows. The only question of interest, it seems to me, is whether its main premise—that maximal greatness *is* possibly instantiated—is *true*. I think it *is* true; hence I think this version of the ontological argument is sound.

But here we must be careful; we must ask whether this argument is a successful piece of natural theology, whether it *proves* the existence of God. And the answer must be, I think, that it does not. An argument for God's existence may be *sound*, after all, without in any useful sense proving God's existence.[24] Since I believe in God, I think the following argument is sound:

> Either God exists or $7 + 5 = 14$
> It is false that $7 + 5 = 14$
> Therefore God exists.

But obviously this isn't a *proof*; no one who didn't already accept the conclusion, would accept the first premise. The ontological argument we've been examining isn't just like this one, of course, but it must be conceded that not everyone who understands and reflects on its central premise—that the existence of a maximally great being is *possible*—will accept it. Still, it is evident, I think, that there is nothing *contrary to reason* or *irrational* in accepting this premise.[25] What I claim for this argument, therefore, is that it establishes, not the *truth* of theism, but its rational acceptability. And hence it accomplishes at least one of the aims of the tradition of natural theology.

24. See George Mavrodes, *Belief in God* (New York: Macmillan Co., 1970), pp. 22ff.
25. For more on this see Plantinga, *The Nature of Necessity*, chap. 10, sec. 8.